Arbeitsblätter

Englische Grammatik
5./6. Schuljahr

43 Arbeitsblätter
für einen kommunikativen Grammatikunterricht

von Detlef und Margaret von Ziegésar

Ernst Klett Sprachen
Stuttgart

Abbildungsnachweise:
Fotos S. 11: TCL / BAVARIA
Fotos S. 53 und 57: dpa

1. Auflage 1 11 10 9 8 | 2013 12 11 10 2009

Alle Drucke dieser Auflage können im Unterricht nebeneinander benutzt werden, sie sind untereinander unverändert. Die letzte Zahl bezeichnet das Jahr dieses Druckes.

www.klett.de

Umschlaggestaltung: BSS Werbeagentur Sachse und Partner, Bietigheim
Illustrationen: Christa Janik, Leinfelden-Echterdingen
Druck: Götz, Ludwigsburg
Printed in Germany.

ISBN 978-3-12-927874-1

9 783129 278741

Simple present

Present continuous

Future

Simple past

Present perfect

Mengenangaben

Steigerung von Adjektiven

Modale Hilfsverben

Allgemeines

Dies ist das erste von drei Arbeitsbüchern zur Übung und Wiederholung von Grammatikstrukturen im Englischunterricht der Sekundarstufe I. Der vorliegende erste Band umfasst das Grammatikpensum der Klassen 5 und 6, der zweite Band enthält die in den Klassen 7 und 8 behandelten Grammatikstrukturen, und der dritte Band übt und wiederholt das Grammatikpensum der Klassen 9 und 10.
Der erste Teil der einzelnen Bände enthält für jede behandelte Grammatikstruktur sorgfältig durchdachte und im Unterricht erprobte Arbeitsblätter. Der zweite Teil stellt detaillierte und übersichtliche didaktisch-methodische Hinweise samt Lösungsvorschlägen zu den Übungen für die Hand der Lehrkraft bereit.
Die Arbeitsbücher können sowohl im Verbund mit einem Lehrwerk als auch lehrbuchunabhängig verwendet werden. Der Wortschatz sowie die Progression der grammatischen Strukturen korrespondieren mit denen der gängigen Englischlehrwerke.
Man kann die Arbeitsbücher in der vorgegebenen Reihenfolge der Strukturen systematisch durchgehen, aber auch je nach Bedarf einzelne Grammatikphänomene herausgreifen.
Die Arbeitsblätter enthalten sowohl mündliche als auch schriftliche Übungen und berücksichtigen die verschiedenen Sozialformen des Unterrichts. Dadurch ist der Einsatz der Arbeitsblätter vielfältig. Es gibt lehrergelenkte Übungen, Gruppen-, Partner- und Projektarbeit. Einzelarbeit ist sowohl in der Klasse als auch zu Hause in Form von Hausaufgaben möglich.

Grammatik

Der vorliegende Band übt und wiederholt die wichtigsten Grammatikphänomene der Klassen 5 und 6 mit strukturierten Materialien in Form von Arbeitsblättern.
Die Arbeitsblätter sind einerseits nach formalgrammatischen Gesichtspunkten geordnet und folgen damit der von den Lehrplänen der verschiedenen Bundesländer vorgeschriebenen und in Lehrwerken verwirklichten Strukturenprogression. Andererseits betten sie die zu übenden Grammatikstrukturen in natürliche Kommunikationsituationen ein und wählen den Strukturen angemessene Textsorten und Themen. Dadurch ist sowohl ein formalgrammatisches Üben und Einschleifen als auch ein kommunikatives Verwenden der Strukturen gewährleistet.
Obwohl der Schwerpunkt der Arbeitsblätter auf dem Üben und Wiederholen von Grammatikstrukturen liegt, werden immer wieder Gelegenheiten zum induktiven Erarbeiten von Grammatikregeln geboten, und Regeln werden in übersichtlichen Merkkästchen zusammengefasst. Die Regeln sind auf Deutsch und in einer schülernahen Sprache verfasst, die den Lernenden vermittelt, dass Regeln nicht um ihrer selbst willen zu lernen sind, sondern als Hilfsmittel zum Erlernen der fremden Sprache.

Textsorten, Themen und Sozialformen

Soweit wie möglich wird mit sprachlich zwar vereinfachten, aber authentischen Textsorten gearbeitet. Es kommen Leserbriefe in Jugendzeitschriften vor (A 2), informative Sachtexte (A 3, A 35, A 41), Fragebögen (A 4, A 20, A 31), Horoskope (A 5), Zeitungsberichte (A 18), Fahrpläne (A 17), Wörterbucheinträge (A 18), Witze (A 4, A 15, A 23, A 24), Schlagzeilen aus Zeitungen (A 30), Notizen (A 10), Fernsehprogramme (A 34), Quizfragen (A 36, A 38) und Werbetexte (A 40). Die Schüler üben und wiederholen in dieser Weise Grammatikstrukturen mit Hilfe von Texten, die ihnen glaubwürdig erscheinen und denen sie in der Realität begegnen können.
Die Themen sind schülernah, indem sie die Erfahrungs- und Interessenlage der Lernenden berücksichtigen und damit die Bereitschaft der Schüler, sich mitzuteilen, nützen. Sie gehen nicht nur auf spezifisch landeskundliche Bereiche der Zielsprachekulturen ein, sondern sind auch von allgemeinem, fächerübergreifendem Interesse, wie z. B. die Themen Umweltprobleme (A 41), bedrohte Tierarten (A 35), zwischenmenschliche Beziehungen (A 2), Freizeitverhalten (A 4), Zukunft und Technologie (A 15), Popmusik (A 19), Gesundheit (A 20), Fernsehen (A 34), allgemeine Informationen

über die Erde (A 36, A 38) und Englisch als Weltsprache (A 1).
Schließlich beziehen die Themen interkulturelle Aspekte mit ein, wie z. B. Lebensweisen und -bedingungen in Ländern zusätzlich zu denen der Zielsprachekulturen, und fördern damit Offenheit in der Begegnung mit Menschen anderer Herkunft.
Interkulturelle Kommunikationskompetenz im Sinne von uneigennützigem Fremdverstehen fängt aber schon im Umgang mit dem nächsten Schüler und beim Verhältnis der Schüler untereinander an. Deshalb wurden neben der Möglichkeit zur lehrerzentrierten und Einzelarbeit sozial-integrative Beziehungsformen wie Partner- und Gruppenarbeit gewählt, die neben dem kognitiven vor allem das soziale Lernen fördern, gleichzeitig die Sprechzeit der Lernenden beträchtlich erweitern und schließlich die Kommunikation wirklichen Wissens und realer Information mit wirklichen Kommunikationspartnern gewährleisten.
Die Begriffe „Schüler“ und „Lehrer“ werden im folgenden als neutrale Sammelbeziehungen verwendet, die jeweils beide Geschlechter umfassen.

1. English is international

People from all over the world speak English.

You: Who's Frank?

Your Partner: He ...

he, she, it – das **s** muss mit!
lives sings
goes teaches

A 1 *Simple present: ‚s‘*

Write what you know about all these people:

Frank __________ in a hotel in Berlin.

Abdul's father ____________________

Donna ____________________

Mona ____________________

Maria ____________________

Mehmet ____________________

Isabella ____________________

Natasha's ____________________

Mike's ____________________

Carlos ____________________

2. Now talk or write about your family

(mother, brother, uncle, cousin ...)

My ____________________

My ____________________

My ____________________

My ____________________

My ____________________

3. Tongue twisters

Say five times:

The sun shine s on shop signs

The swan swims

YOUR LETTERS

Problems with other people? Maybe I can help.

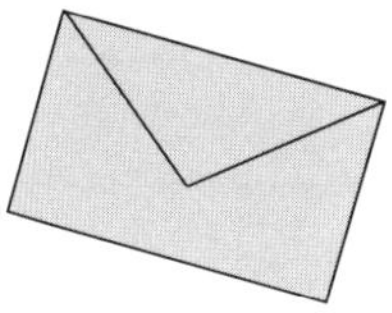

Dear Alison,
I have a problem with my brothers. They don't help with the cleaning at home. So I have to do it.
Barbara

I'm worried about my sister. She doesn't eat fruit and she doesn't do sports. It's not very good for her. **Sue**

My parents don't know my friends, but they don't like them.
John

My friend doesn't listen to me.
Jenny

My friend takes my comics. But he doesn't bring them back.
Steve

My little brother doesn't have any hobbies. He only watches TV all the time. I'm worried about him.
Tony

My parents don't like my hair.
Barry

My friend uses my things. But she doesn't ask me first.
Helen

My sister doesn't feed our hamster. And she doesn't clean its cage. It's always me. **Frank**

My friend's hair looks awful. But I don't want to tell her.
Maria

I/You/We/They	**don't help** with the cleaning.
He/She/It (the cat)	**doesn't eat** fruit.

don't = do not
doesn't = does not

1. Who has a problem with ...?

brothers or sisters	parents	friends?
______	______	______
______	______	______
______	______	______
______	______	______

2. What are their problems?

Brothers or sisters:

Barbara's brothers ______________________________ home.

Tony's ______________________________ hobbies.

Sue's ______________________________

____

Frank's ______________________________

______________________________ cage.

Parents:

Barry's ______________________________

John's ______________________________

Friends:

Helen's friend ______________ But ______________

Jenny's ______________________________

Steve's ______________________________

____

Maria's friend's hair ______________ But Maria ______________

____

3. And you? Have you any problems with people?

Write two down:

My _____ **doesn't** _____ **don't** _____

1. ______________________________
2. ______________________________

4. Which of these things don't you do? And your friend?

collect stamps/ ...	listen to	want to
drink tea/ ...	play the piano/ ...	watch much TV
eat hamburgers/ ...	play football/ ...	watch horror films
go to pop concerts	read comics/thrillers	watch programmes about
have a pet/computer/...	read books about	write letters

1. I **don't** collect ______________ My friend **doesn't** collect ______________
2. ______________ He/She ______________
3. ______________ ______________
4. ______________ ______________
5. ______________ ______________

Indian elephant

Animals

Elephants live in Africa and Asia. They don't eat meat. They drink a lot of water. People sometimes kill them for their tusks.

The Indian elephant is smaller. It doesn't have big ears like the African elephant.

African elephant

1. Find the right sentences

comes
doesn't eat
don't eat
doesn't have
doesn't sleep
don't sleep
drink
lives
sleep
sleeps

Elephants	drink	in the day.
The Indian elephant	________	people.
Elephants	________	a lot of water.
Hamsters	________	big ears.
Guinea pigs	________	at night.
The hedgehog	________	from Africa and Asia.
The frog	________	meat.
The elephant	________	in the day.
The jaguar	________	in winter.
The killer whale	________	in South America.

2. Let's write about some animals

Elephants ________ a lot of water. But they ________ (not drink) through their noses or 'trunks'.

The Indian elephant ________ (not have) big ears.

Crocodiles ________ meat. They ________ (not live) on land.

The giraffe ________ a long neck. It ________ (not eat) meat.

The kangaroo ________ in Australia. It ________ (not live) in Europe.

Elephants, hamsters, guinea pigs, hedgehogs, jaguars and whales ________ warm blood. So they are 'mammals'. Frogs and fish ________ (not have) warm blood.

A 4 *Simple present: Wh*-Fragen mit *do*

1. What do you know about your partner?

QUESTIONNAIRE

My partner's name: ______________________

1. What do you do when you're not at school? ______________________

____

2. What books do you read? (adventure/detective stories/books about) ______________________

____

3. Which TV programmes do you watch? ______________________

4. Which group or singer do you like best? ______________________

5. What do you think about sports? ______________________

____

6. How do you feel about school? ______________________

____

7. What do you want to be when you leave school? (Maybe/don't know yet) ______________________

____

8. Which places do you want to see? ______________________

Ask your partner question 1 and write down the answer.
Now your partner asks you question 1 and writes down your answer.

2. Exchange sheets

Pick out a question that interests you, for example:

What books	**do you**	read?
What books	**does he**	read?

My partner's name: *Jochen*
2. What books do you read?

Now ask the class to guess what's on the sheet: What books **does** Jochen read?

3. Can you find the joke?

1. Where/come/do/from/pencils?

______________________?

Pennsylvania!

2. Where/dance/snowmen/do?

______________________?

At a snowball

1. Are horoscopes always right?

Aquarius (Jan 21 - Feb 19)
Aquarians always have lots of friends. They are always happy.

Pisces (Feb 20 - March 20)
These people always want to do new things. They never work very hard. But they are never unhappy.

Aries (March 21 - April 20)
Aries people always have a lot of fun. But they sometimes work hard, too.

Taurus (April 21 - May 22)
Taurus people sometimes have very good ideas. They often want to know things. They are sometimes unhappy.

Gemini (May 23 - June 21)
These people never listen to others. They are often unhappy.

Cancer (June 22 - July 22)
Cancer people often think about things. They never do anything fast.

Leo (July 23 - Aug 22)
Leo people always have fun. They are never unhappy.

Virgo (Aug 23 - Sept 22)
These people never want to do anything new. They often stay at home.

Libra (Sept 23 - Oct 22)
Librans often help others. They never talk about their problems.

Scorpio (Oct 23 - Nov 21)
Scorpions sometimes talk about other people. That's why they sometimes have problems with them.

Sagittarius (Nov 22 - Dec 22)
Sagittarians always talk a lot. They are sometimes unhappy.

Capricorn (Dec 23 - Jan 20)
These people often think about problems. They always ask a lot of questions.

What's the same?

1. Aries and Leo people ____
2. Pisces and Leo people ______________ un ______________________
3. Aquarian and Leo people ______________ h ______________________
4. Taurus people __________________________ things. And Capricorn people

   ____
5. Cancer and Capricorn people __________________________ about things.

What's different?

1. Pisces people ____

   But Virgo people ____
2. Pisces ____

   But Aries ____
3. Aquarians ____

   But Gemini people ____
4. Gemini people __________________________________ others.

   Librans __________________________________ others.

2. When's your birthday?

When's your birthday, Danny?
On Aug 25.
So you're Virgo. You never want to do anything new. Is that right?
No, that's rubbish.
And you often stay at home.
Well, I sometimes stay at home, but not often.

And you? What sort of person are you?

I (always/sometimes/often/never)

____

____

____

And your friend, your sister or your brother?

My ____________ (always/sometimes/...)

____

____

____

What I think about horoscopes

I always/sometimes/often/never read .../ I (don't) think/(don't) believe in them/because .../ My horoscope says ..., but .../(not)true/...

____

____

3. Translate these sentences

a) Aquarians *always have* a lot of friends. — Wassermänner ______________________

____

b) Pisces people *never work* very hard. — Fische ______________________

Im **Englischen** stehen *always, sometimes, often, never* .... (vor, hinter) Vollverben wie *have, work.*	Die entsprechenden **deutschen** Wörter stehen dagegen .... (vor, hinter) dem Vollverb.

Suche weitere Beispiele aus den Horoskopen: *(always ...)* + **Vollverb**:

____

c) Aquarians *are always* happy. ______________________

d) Pisces people *are never* unhappy. ______________________

Im **Englischen wie im Deutschen** stehen solche Wörter (*always* ...) ...... (vor, hinter) dem Hilfsverb *be*/sein.

Suche weitere Beispiele aus den Horoskopen. ______________________

1. Do you collect anything?

Ask your partner these questions and fill in his or her answers:

	Yes	No
Do you collect anything?	*stamps*	
Do you do any sports?		
Do you like music?		
Do you play any instruments?		
Do you read books, comics or magazines?		
Do you have brothers or sisters?		
Do you have a pet?		

2. Children in other countries

Joe comes from Zimbabwe, a country in the south-east of Africa. This is how his day starts.

5.30 I get up and put on my school uniform. I walk 5 kilometres to school.

7.30 Lessons start. There are 50 pupils in a class and one book for 2 pupils.

Do I/you/we/they know anything about Zimbabwe?

Find out more about Joe and his country.

Do all children **go** to school?	No, some have to work.
... they all ... to go to school? (want)	Yes, of course. They want to learn to read and write.

Your partner is Joe. Ask him 5 questions:		**Your partner:**
... to school in the afternoons?	*do*	Yes. We work in the school garden.
... sports?	*eat*	Sometimes we play football.
... hamburgers or chips?	*go*	No. They're too expensive.
... people ... telephones?	*watch*	Only in the towns.
... people ... TV in the evenings?	*have*	No. They work in the house.

Now you are Joe and your partner asks you:		
... people ... things in shops?	*have*	No, mostly in markets.
... most people ... in towns or villages?	*buy*	In villages.
... most people ... cars?	*live*	No. They use buses.
... young people ... to discos?	*live*	There are no discos?
... young people ... with their parents?	*go*	Yes, of course.

1. Which girl is my sister?

Diane

- plays table-tennis
- collects stamps and posters
- reads books

Carol

- plays the guitar
- collects posters
- reads books
- plays table-tennis

Linda

- plays the guitar
- reads comics
- plays table-tennis
- collects stamps
- and posters

Sue

- collects stamps
- reads comics
- plays the guitar

Which is my sister? Can you guess?

- Does she read comics?
  No, she doesn't.
- Does she play the guitar?
  Yes, she does.
- Then it's Carol.

Does + Grundform

Doe(s) she **collect** stamps?

‚s' ist schon da – deshalb hier kein ‚s' mehr.

Does he/she/it		**like** chips?
Do I/you/we/they		

2. A quiz

Partner A

Ask your partner these questions. Give him or her one point for every correct answer.

1. Does *homework* mean "Hausarbeit" or "Hausaufgaben"?
2. Do we say *I do my homework* or *I make my homework*?
3. Do you say *I'm living in Germany* or *I live in Germany*?
4. Does *chips* mean "Chips" or "Pommes frites"?
5. Do British children go to school in the afternoons?
6. Do British children go to school on Saturdays?
7. Does a British person get Christmas presents on 24 Dec or 25 Dec?
8. Does someone from Cardiff live in Scotland or Wales?
9. Do they play football or tennis at Wembley?
10. Does the Prime Minister live in Buckingham Palace?

Partner B

Ask your partner these questions. Give him or her one point for every correct answer.

1. Does *TV programme* mean "Fernsehsendung" or "Fernsehprogramm"?
2. Do we ask *How much costs it?* or *How much does it cost?*
3. Does "ich will" mean *I will* or *I want?*
4. Do most English schools start at eight or nine o'clock?
5. Do most English schools finish at one or four in the afternoon?
6. Does Father Christmas come to British children on 6 Dec, 24 Dec or 25 Dec?
7. Does someone from Belfast live in Scotland or Northern Ireland?
8. Does *British* mean the same as *English*?
9. Does the Queen live in the Houses of Parliament?
10. Do they play football or tennis at Wimbledon?

1. Who has a pet?

Who **has** a pet?	
Who	**likes animals?**
	reads magazines?
	watches films?
	collects things?
	likes music?
	goes to a club?
	plays an instrument?

What kind **do you have?**		
What	**do you**	**like?**
		read?
		watch?
		collect?
Which (group)		like?
		go to?
		play?

pets	animals	magazines	films
______	______	______	______
______	______	______	______
What kind?	What kind?	What kind?	What kind?
______	______	______	______
______	______	______	______
______	______	______	______
______	______	______	______
______	______	______	______
______	______	______	______

collect	music	club	instrument
______	______	______	______
______	______	______	______
What?	Which group?	Which?	Which?
______	______	______	______
______	______	______	______
______	______	______	______
______	______	______	______
______	______	______	______
______	______	______	______

2. Can you remember your questions?

pets:	**Who has** a pet?	What kind **do** you **have?**
animals:	______________ animals?	What kind ______________ ?
collect:	______________ things?	What ______________ ?
club:	______________ a club?	Which club ______________ ?
	Bei diesen Fragen interessieren wir uns für das **Subjekt** des Satzes. (Das Subjekt tut etwas). Daher **kein** *do.*	Hier fragen wir nicht nach dem Subjekt, sondern nach *etwas anderem,* (**was** jemand sammelt, nicht wer sammelt; **wohin** jemand geht). Daher brauchen wir *do.*

What goes up and down, but never moves?
(Stairs.)

Woman in shoe shop: I'd like a pair of crocodile shoes, please.
Assistant: Of course, madam.
What size **does** your crocodile **take**?

3. Who likes Pedro?

Who *likes* Pedro? Jackie.
Who **does** Pedro **like**? Angela.

1. Who *likes* Angela?
2. Who **does** Angela **like**?
3. Who likes Barry?
4. Who does Barry like?

Go on with the questions.

5. Who ______________________________ ?
6. ______________________________ ?
7. ______________________________ ?
8. ______________________________ ?
9. ______________________________ ?
10. ______________________________ ?

B	A	R	R	Y	
H	A	S	S	A	N
C	A	R	O	L	
J	A	C	K	I	E
H	A	S	S	A	N
P	E	D	R	O	

1. What's the time?

8.00	9.00	12.00	16.00	23.00
Stuttgart	Ankara	Delhi	Tokyo	San Francisco

Annette

Kemal and Nuray

Hassan and Ali

Mr Chang

Mrs Webb

1. It is **8.00** in Stuttgart. Annette **is** just gett**ing** up.
   In Ankara it is **9.00**. Kemal and Nuray **are** work**ing**.

a) In Delhi it is **12.00**.

Hassan and Ali ______________ (have lunch).

b) In Tokyo it is [ ].

Mr Chang ______________ (go home).

c) In San Francisco ______________ [ ].

Mrs ______________ (go to bed).

> Wir beschreiben, was jemand **in diesem Moment gerade** tut:
>
> | | |
> |---|---|
> | He/She/It **is** | work**ing**. |
> | You/We/They **are** | hav**ing** lunch. |

2. It is **12.00** in Stuttgart. Annette ______________ (shop).

a) In Ankara it is [ ]. Kemal and Nuray ______________ (have lunch).

b) In Delhi it is [ ]. Hassan and Ali ______________ (go home).

c) In Tokyo it is [ ]. Mr Chang ______________ (watch TV).

3. It is **5.00** in Stuttgart. Annette ______________ (sleep).

a) In Ankara it is [ ]. ______________ (get up).

b) In Delhi ______ [ ]. ______________ (go to work).

c) In Tokyo ______ [ ]. ______________ (have lunch).

d) In San Francisco ______ [ ]. ______________ (read a book).

2. And your family? Your friends?

What do you think?

Just now I think my ... is/are ...ing

At this moment everyone in the world is doing the same thing. What is it?
Getting older

1. Brighton in summer

Kevin works for a Brighton newspaper. He wants to find out what all these people are doing in Brighton.

Paul Alain Trevor Gudrun Pete

Sue Carol Lisa Chris Dave Barbara Jill

These are his notes. What did he find out?

Alain - learn English	Alain ______________________ English.
Gudrun - stay with penfriend	Gudrun ______________________
Carol and Pete - visit friends	Carol and ______________________
Barbara and Jill - look for job	______________________
Sue and Dave - work in hotel	______________________
Lisa - take photos for magazine	______________________
Chris and Paul - play in band	______________________
Trevor - interview tourists	______________________

I'**m** learn**ing** English.
We'**re** work**ing** in a hotel.

Mit solchen **-ing**-Formen zeigen wir, dass eine Tätigkeit **angefangen** hat und **noch nicht zu Ende** ist. Sie muss nicht unbedingt gerade jetzt im Moment ablaufen.

2. Memory game

Find a partner. Test his or her memory.

You:
1. Alain's working in a hotel.
2. Gudrun is looking for a job.
3. Trevor is interviewing tourists.
4. Sue and Dave are playing in a band.

Now your partner tests you:

Your partner:
5. Lisa's taking photos for a magazine.
6. Chris and Paul are learning English.
7. Barbara and Jill are working in a hotel.
8. Barbara is staying with her penfriend.

Your partner:
That's right/wrong.
He's (not) ...ing ... (He's ...).

You/We/They	**aren't** **'re not**	learn**ing** English.
He/She/It	**isn't** **'s not**	learn**ing** English.

1. Let's draw some pictures

Draw these pictures in the boxes. In some pictures two people do the same thing. Don't show your pictures to your partner.

Linda	Sue and Andy	Tony	John and Dave
Ann and Martin	Barbara	Paul	Sally and Tina

Is Linda ...**ing**?	Yes, she is/No, she isn't.
Are Sue and Andy ...**ing**?	Yes, they are/No, they aren't/they're not.

2. What are you doing here?

Make up dialogues like this:

– What are you doing here in (Milan/London/Berlin/Scotland/...)?

– I'm (visiting friends/learning English/working in ...).

– And where are you staying?

– In a (hotel/youth hostel/with friends/on a camp site/...).

3. What are they doing here?

Cover your work sheet up so your partner can't see your box.

What is/are ... doing in Karlsruhe?
Where is/are ... staying?

Partner A

	Tony	Georgio/Anna	Rita	Mr and Mrs Betts
doing in Karlsruhe?	?	working in a cafe	?	sightseeing
staying?	?	with friends	?	in a hotel

Partner B

	Tony	Georgio/Anna	Rita	Mr and Mrs Betts
doing in Karlsruhe?	learning German	?	looking for a job	?
staying?	with his penfriend	?	at a youth hostel	?

1. American Indians

Dorothy is an American Indian, a Hopi. She is telling some tourists about life on the Indian reservation.
Read what she says and try to name the people in the pictures.
Describe the pictures.

Dorothy is making a rug.

a) ______________________

Dorothy: Sarah and I make rugs. Sarah isn't making one right now. Today she's making bread.

We sell the rugs at our tourist center. Mike takes them there for us. He works at the center. But today he's at home. He's making jewelry.

Maria usually makes bread. But today she's helping Susanna to make baskets.

We also have fields. Ben and Adam are working in the fields behind our caravans. They're planting corn.

We have a school on the reservation. My daughter, Anna, goes there. But they're on holiday today. She's riding her motorbike.

b) ______________________

d) ______________________

c) ______________________

e) ______________________

Lies noch einmal Dorothys Bericht und unterstreiche mit verschiedenen Farben alle Verben im *simple present* und *present continuous.* Kannst du die folgenden Regeln vervollständigen?

Wir verwenden das *simple present* für Dinge, die man ______________________

______________________ z.B. ______________________

Wir verwenden das *present continuous* für Dinge, die man ______________________

______________________ z.B. ______________________

2. Life on the reservation

You are talking to the Indians. What do they tell you? Use the *simple present* or *present continuous.*

Maria

Well, you see that *I'm making* baskets today. *I don't* normally *make* baskets, but today I ______________ Susanna (help). Usually I ______________ bread (make). Sarah ______________ it today (make). Sometimes tourists ______________ and we ______________ it to them (come, sell).

Mike

I ______________ at the tourist center three days a week (work). We ______________ jewelry, rugs and baskets (sell). Right now I ______________ jewelry (make). The women always ______________ the rugs and baskets (make). When they're finished I ______________ them to the center (take).

Ben

I ______________ in the fields every day (work). It's hard, but I ______________ it (like).

Which words told you that you needed the *simple present* or *present continuous*?

3. What I know about American Indians

Write what you can remember about American Indians.
These words will help you: *have – help – live – make – plant – sell – work.*

The Hopis ______________ in caravans on a reservation. They ______________ things and ______________ them at their tourist center. Dorothy and Sarah ______________ rugs, but today Sarah ______________________ . Mike usually ______________ at the tourist centre, but right now he ______________________________ . Maria usually ______________ bread, but today she ______________ to make baskets. The Indians also ______________ fields. Today Ben and Adam ______________ in the fields. They ______________________________ .

What else would you like to know about American Indians?
Write down some questions. How much information can you find?

1. What's going to happen?

Complete these sentences. This box will help you.
Use: *break, close, cross drop, fall, miss, pass, win.*

He's not He isn't They're not They aren't	**going to**	come.

1.  It's g __________ to rain.

2.  She __________ into the water.

3.  They __________ the sofa.

4. 

Arsenal __________ the match.

5. 

They __________ the bus.

6.  They __________ the bridge.

7. 

The factory __________

8. 

She __________ the maths exam.

9.  They __________ the window.

Überlege, weshalb wir immer *going to* verwendet haben.

Wir verwenden *going to* __________

____

A 14 *Future: going to* (Absichten, Pläne)

1. I'm going to ...

I'm going to lie in the sun this afternoon.

And you?

I 'm going to ...

2. Are you going to ...?

Interview your partner: Ask five questions and note down the answers.
Start with your partner's name. Use *going to* or *not going to.*

Are you going to play football today?

I don't know yet.

do sports	go shopping
listen to	play
ride	see a friend
watch	go to
	write ...

1. ______________ is ______________________________

2. He/She ______________________________

3. ______________________________

4. ______________________________

5. ______________________________

Now your partner asks you five questions.

Überlege, weshalb wir immer *going to* verwendet haben.

Wir haben immer *going* to benutzt, weil es sich um ______________ handelt.

3. Holiday plans

Andy, Barbara and Jackie want to take these things on holiday with them. What are their plans?

Andy is going to ______________________

He ______________________

____

____

Barbara and Jackie are g ______________________

They ______________________

____

____

1. 100 YEARS FROM NOW

What do you think life will be like in your country a hundred years from now?

1. Where will most people live?
   a) In houses.
   b) In flats.
   c) In towns.
   d) In villages.
   e) On other planets.

2. Where will most people work?
   a) In offices.
   b) In factories.
   c) At home.
   d) On other planets.
   e) People won't work more than 25 hours a week.

3. What will schools be like?
   a) Children will still go to school.
   b) Every pupil will probably have a computer at school.
   c) Children will not have to go to school.

4. What will the traffic be like?
   a) There will probably be more cars and roads.
   b) All cars will be electric.
   c) People won't use cars any more.
   d) People won't be allowed to use cars.

5. What will life at home be like?
   a) People won't have to do any cleaning.
   b) Robots will do the cooking.
   c) People probably won't eat normal food.
   d) There won't be more than two children in the family.
   e) When we phone someone we will see them, too.

6. What will the world look like?
   a) There probably won't be any trees.
   b) There will be more trees.
   c) Countries next to the sea won't exist. They will be under the sea.

2. Will/won't

Könntest du erklären, warum wir hier *will* bzw. *will not/won't* gebrauchen?

Für Dinge, die ______________________

____

____

People	**will**	live ...
Children	**will not**	go ...
There	**won't**	be ...

Meistens **schreibt** man: **will**
Meistens **spricht** man: **'ll**
aber nicht nach [l]: *people will*

	1	2	
There	**will**	**probably**	be more cars.

	2	1	
There	**probably**	**won't**	be any trees.

probably steht **vor** *won't*

Aufgepasst!

I **will** – Ich *werde*
Ich *will* – I **want**

3. Translate into German

A hundred years from now *there probably won't be* any trees.

____

Schau die unterstrichenen Wörter an. Worin unterscheidet sich deine Übersetzung? Im Deutschen ist es meist unwichtig, ob wir das Präsens *(gibt)* oder das Futur (*wird es ... geben*) benutzen. Im Englischen dagegen muss man das *will-future* verwenden.

4. My ideas about the future

Use these words, but write down your own ideas, too.

will | on the moon | travel to/by | won't | have to | do | Robots

Most people ______ live ______________________

They ______ ______________________

______ ______ ______________________

______ ______ ______________________

______ ______ ______________________

______ ______ ______________________

______ ______ ______________________

______ ______ ______________________

______ ______ ______________________

5. Can you match these jokes?

1. Teacher: In the exam you will have five minutes for every question.
2. Customer in cafe: Waiter, I don't like the flies in here.
   (fly - *Fliege*)
3. Waiter, will the pancakes be long?
   (pancake - *Pfannkuchen*)
4. Do you think I'll lose my looks when I get older?
   (looks - *gutes Aussehen*)

a) No, round.

b) And how long will we have for the answers?

c) Hopefully.

d) Come again tomorrow. We'll have new ones then.

1. ______ 2. ______ 3. ______ 4. ______

Teacher: What are you making, Steve?
Steve: A liquid that will dissolve anything.
Teacher: And what will you keep it in?
liquid - Flüssigkeit, dissolve - auflösen, keep - aufbewahren

1. How can these people help?

Use *I'll carry, get, go and ask, help, take, shut.*

Im Deutschen verwenden wir das **Präsens**. Ich *helfe* dir.	Im Englischen brauchen wir **will:** I'*ll help* you.

Wann gebrauchen wir „**I'll**"?

Wenn wir spontan ______________________________

2. What do you say?

Partner A

Can someone check my homework, please?

I need some stamps.

My anorak's upstairs.

My train arrives at half past six.

I've left my exercise-book at home.

I'm late for school.

I'm hungry.

There's been an accident.

I'd like a coke.

I want to go to town this afternoon.

It's our teacher's birthday on Monday.

It's hot in here.

Partner B

I'll get you a sandwich.
I'll get you some when I go out.
I'll do it.
I'll buy you one.
I'll phone for an ambulance.
I'll make a cake.
I'll take you on my bike.
I'll get it for you.
I'll open the window.
I'll give you some paper.
I'll meet you at the station.
I'll come with you.

1. Travelling to Germany

Jean, from London, is going to see her penfriend in Karlsruhe.
Andy, from Dover, is going to stay with his uncle in Cologne.
How will they get there?

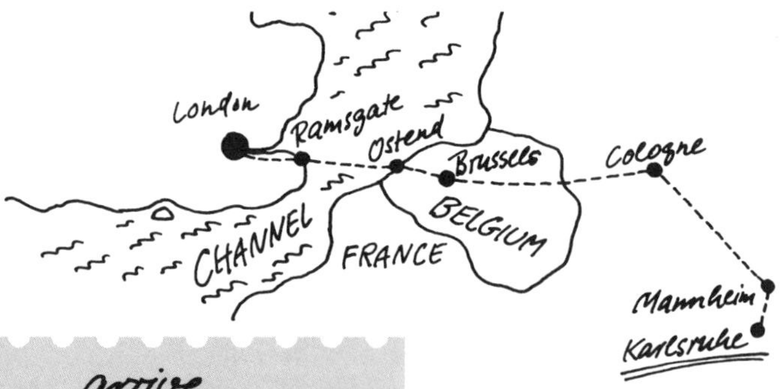

leave	arrive
London-bus to station, Sat. 6.50	7.10
Train from London 7.25	Ramsgate 8.15
Ferry from Ramsgate 9.30	Ostend 14.00
Train from Ostend 14.30	Mannheim 22.30
Train from Mannheim 23.30	Karlsruhe 1.30

Will (she, he, it, they) fly?
No, (she, he, it, they) **won't.** **Yes,** (she, he, it, they) **will.**

1. Will Jean go to the station by taxi?
   No, she won't. She'll go by bus.
2. Will she go to Ramsgate by train?
   Yes, she will.
3. Will they fly across the Channel? No, ___ They ___
   ___
4. Will the ferry arrive in Ostend in the morning? ___
   It ___
5. Will the ferry land in Germany? ___ It ___
   ___
6. Will Jean have to change trains? ___ – in ___
7. Will Andy have to change trains? ___
8. Will Jean arrive in Karlsruhe on Saturday? ___ She ___
   ___

2. What are the questions?

Use *What – When – What time – How – How long?*

1. How will Jean get to the station? – By bus.
2. ___ she get to Ramsgate? – By train.
3. ___ she arrive in Ramsgate? – At 8.15.
4. ___ they be on the boat? – For four and a half hours.
5. ___ they get to Germany from Ostend? – By train.

1. Using your dictionary

Lies diesen Zeitungsausschnitt und unterstreiche die Wörter, die du nicht verstehst.

> Yesterday afternoon a masked man stole £ 500 from a shop. When he left the shop a little dog ran after him and held onto his trouser leg. Because of the dog the police could catch the thief.

steak **545** **step**

sichtig! **III** *s sl* fester Freund, feste Freundin; **IV** *tr* beruhigen; ausgleichen; ▶ ~ **o.s.** festen Halt finden; **V** *itr* sich beruhigen; ruhiger werden.
steak [steɪk] **1.** Steak *n;* **2.** (Fisch)Filet *n.*
steal [sti:l] ‹*irr* stole, stolen› **I** *tr* stehlen *a. fig;* ▶ ~ **s.th. from s.o.** jdm etw stehlen; ~ **a march on s.o.** jdm zuvorkommen; ~ **a glance at s.o.** verstohlen zu jdm hinschauen; ~ **the show** die Schau stehlen; **II** *itr* **1.** stehlen; **2.** sich stehlen, sich schleichen; ▶ ~ **away** sich wegstehlen; ~ **about** herumschleichen; ~ **up on s.o.** sich an jdn heranschleichen; **III** *s Am fam* Geschenk *n.*
stealth [stelθ] List *f;* ▶ **by** ~ durch List; **stealthy** ['stelθɪ] *adj* heimlich, verstohlen.
lassen; ▶ **be ~ed in s.th.** von etw durchdrungen sein; **~ed in ignorance** durch und durch unwissend.
steepen ['sti:pən] **I** *tr* steiler machen; **II** *itr* steiler werden.
steeple ['sti:pl] Kirchturm *m;* **steeple-chase** [—tʃeɪs] **1.** *(Pferde)* Hindernisrennen *n;* **2.** *(Leichtathletik) sport* Hindernislauf *m;* **steeple·chaser** [—ə(r)] *(Pferd)* **1.** Steepler; *(Jockey)* Reiter(in) *m (f)* in einem Hindernisrennen; **2.** *(Leichtathletik)* Hindernisläufer(in) *m (f).*
steer[1] [stɪə(r)] **I** *tr* **1.** steuern *a. fig;* **2.** *fig* lenken, leiten, führen; ▶ ~ **a course for s.th.** *fig* auf etw zusteuern; **II** *itr* lenken; steuern; ~ **due south** Kurs nach Süden halten; ~ **for s.th.** etw ansteuern; auf

Wo schaust du im Wörterbuch nach, um die Bedeutung der folgenden Wörter zu finden?

stole – ________ , *left* – ________ *ran* – ________ , *held* – ________ , *could* – ________

Bei *simple past*-Formen muss ich die ________ formen nachschlagen.

> Wir erzählen, was zu **einem bestimmten Zeitpunkt** in der **Vergangenheit** passiert. ⟶ Wir brauchen *simple past*-Formen

2. ‚Simple past'-Formen

Kennst du die *simple past*-Formen dieser Verben?

Regelmäßige Verben *(regular verbs)*	
Grundform	*simple past*
work	work**ed**
help	________
play	________
want	________
like	________
phone	________
stop	________ (!)
try	________ (!)

Bei **regelmäßigen** Verben *(regular verbs)* hängt man einfach - ________ an die ________ form.

Unregelmäßige Verben *(irregular verbs)*	
Grundform	*simple past*
have	**had**
be	________
go	________
get	________
make	________
ride	________
see	________
take	________

Die *simple past*-Formen von **unregelmäßigen** Verben *(irregular verbs)* muss man auswendig lernen!

3. Indian 'books'

Before there were books people told stories in pictures.
Can you read these stories about American Indians? (You need *simple past*-forms.)

1.

Red Foot **went** to the river to fish. He **fell** into the water.

He ________ swim (cannot). Silver Hand ________ Red Foot's pony (see).

He ________ the pony (take). He ________ the pony next to the river (ride).

He ________ Red Foot (find). He ________ Red Foot out of the river (pull).

They ________ home together (ride).

2.

Black Leg ________ to the woods to find food (go). He ________ down and ________ his leg (fall, break). He ________ walk (cannot). Big Man ________ his bag (see).

He ________ Black Leg (find). He ________ him something to drink (give).

Then he ________ back to the village to get help (ride).

3.

Brown Bear ________ to the mountains to look for food (go). He ________ into a hole (fall). He ________ get out (cannot). Little Foot ________ (see).

He ________ Brown Bear (find). He ________ him out of ________ ________ (pull). They ________ (ride).

And your story?

Draw pictures and write about what you did:

Last night/Yesterday/On holiday ...

1. Wanda, the pop star

Today Wanda is a pop star. People all over the world know her. She is rich and can have anything she wants.
Ten years ago Wanda's name was Wendy. She didn't have much money and life was very difficult.

TEN YEARS AGO	TODAY
She __________ to parties.	She goes to a party every week.
She __________ many clothes.	She can buy lots of clothes.
She __________ much.	She can travel all over the world.
She __________ any pop stars.	She knows hundreds of pop stars.
She __________ on holiday.	She goes on two holidays a year.
She __________ in hotels.	She stays in hotels.
She __________ German.	She can speak German and French.
She ____________________	She can dance beautifully.
She __________ any instruments.	She plays the guitar and the piano.
She __________ many people.	She meets hundreds of people.
She __________ many letters.	She gets hundreds of letters.
People __________ interested in her.	People are very interested in her.
She __________ very fit.	She is very fit. She jogs every day.
She __________ very happy.	She is very happy.

	didn't / couldn't + Grundform	
I / You / They He / She / It We / They	**didn't know** **couldn't speak**	any pop stars. English.

be
She **wasn't** very happy. People **weren't** interested.

2. And you?

What didn't or couldn't you do five years ago?

1. Five years ago I ______________________________

2. I ______________________________

3. ______________________________

1. A HEALTH QUIZ

How healthy are you? Let's look at what you did yesterday. Ask your partner these questions.

	Yes, I did	No, I didn't
1. Did you walk to school yesterday?	☐	☐
2. Did you go to school by bike?	☐	☐
2. Did you eat any fruit?	☐	☐
3. Did you eat any chocolates or sweets?	☐	☐
4. Did you have more than one cup of tea or coffee?	☐	☐
5. Did you drink any fruit juice?	☐	☐
6. Did you do any sports?	☐	☐
7. Did you watch TV for more than two hours?	☐	☐
8. Did you go to bed after ten?	☐	☐

Now your partner asks you the questions.

Did	you	**walk** **eat**	to school yesterday? any fruit?

Yes, No,	I/we/she/they/...	**did.** **didn't.**

2. Stop, thief!

When Paul came in an hour ago his flat looked like this. Inspector Watson has to ask some questions. What does she ask? What does Paul answer? Use *was* or *were.*

Was	I/he/she/it	at home?
Yes, No,	I/he/she/it	**was.** **wasn't.**

Were	you/we/they/	at home?
Yes, No,	you/we/they/	**were.** **weren't.**

__________ you out for long?	No, I __________ Only an hour.
__________ the windows open?	No, they __________
__________ the chair under the window?	Yes, __________
__________ these clothes on the floor?	Yes, __________
__________ this knife on the table?	No, __________
__________ the wardrobe doors open?	No, __________

Where is the thief?

1. Find the jokes

1. What did one ghost say to the other?
2. What did Big Chief Running Water* call his two sons?
3. How did you find the weather when you were on holiday?
4. Why did the pioneers cross America in waggons?
5. What did one wall say to the other?
6. How did the accident happen?

*fließendes Wasser

– Hot and cold.
– They didn't want to wait 40 years for a train.
– A sign said STOP! LOOK! And while I did the bus hit me.
– Let's meet at the corner.
– Do you believe in people?
– I just went outside and there it was.

Weißt du, wie man solche Fragen bildet?

Fragewort + *did* ________________ ? (Grundform oder *simple past*-Form)?

What	**did**	the ghost ....? (say, said)
When	**did**	you ....? (arrive, arrived)
Where	**did**	they ....? (go, went)

2. Did you like London?

Your partner went to London last year. You are very interested. Ask questions like this:

When **did** you ...? Where

1. When did you go to London?
2. Where - stay?
3. How - get there?
4. How long - stay in London?
5. How - get around?
6. What - see?
7. What - eat?
8. What - do at night?
9. How many photos - take?
10. What - like best?

Now answer your partner's questions.

You went to London last year. Your partner is very interested and asks you lots of questions. Answer:

(...) = you can say something else.

1. In the summer holidays (...).
2. With my penfriend/In a hotel (...).
3. By train to Ostend, then by ferry to Ramsgate, then by train to London.(...).
4. For two weeks. (...).
5. By bus and underground.
6. Tower Bridge, Buckingham Palace (...).
7. Oh, lots of good things. (...).
8. Played games, mostly. (...).
9. Oh, hundreds! (...).
10. Everything. London's fantastic! (...)

Now you ask the questions.

3. What were the questions?

How long - you on the boat? *(be)* – For four and a half hours.

What - it like in London? *(be)* – Great!

Wir brauchen kein *did* beim Verb .....

A 22 Simple past: Wh-Fragen (*Who painted ...? / What did he paint ...?*)

1. A quiz

1. Who was the first man on the moon?
2. Who painted the 'Mona Lisa'?
3. Where did the summer Olympic Games take place in 2000?
4. When did Columbus go to America?
5. What kind of novels did Agatha Christie write?
6. Who was Sherlock Holmes?
7. Which city had the first underground railway?
8. Which country made paper first?
9. Which language did the Romans speak?
10. What was Boris Becker good at?

Can you tell me what happened in 1779?
- I don't even know what happened last night!

2. Questions! Questions! Questions!

Fragewort + *simple past*	**Fragewort + did + Grundwort**
a) Who *painted* the Mona Lisa? b) What *happened* last night?	a) What *did* da Vinci paint? b) Where *did* it happen?
Mit diesem Fragetyp fragen wir nach dem **Subjekt** (**Wer** hat etwas gemacht? **Was** ist passiert?)	Mit diesem Fragetyp fragen wir nach **anderen Dingen** (**Was** hat jemand gemacht? **Wo/Wann/Wie** ist etwas passiert?)

Welche Fragen muss man stellen, um folgende Antworten zu bekommen?
In jedem Satzpaar brauchst du einmal die Grundform des Verbs und einmal die *simple past*-Form.

the hamster – the snake – eat – ate

What did the snake eat ______? The hamster.

What ate ______? The snake.

Latin – the Romans – speak – spoke

1. Wh ____ ______________? The Romans.

2. Wh ____ ______________? Latin.

America – go – went

3. Wh ____ ______________ first? Columbus.

4. When ______________? In 1492.

Austria – famous musician – Mozart – live – lived

5. Which ______________? Mozart.

6. Wh ____ ______________? In Austria.

1. What has happened?

drop

He **has dropped** his ice-cream.
(Wir schreiben ‚He **has** dropped', aber wir sagen ‚**He's** dropped'.)

1. 

eat

____

__________ too much cake.

2. 

break

____

____

3. 

kick

____

____

4. 

fall off

____

____

5. 

make

____

__________ model ship.

6. 

jump

____

____

7. 

see

____

__________ ghost.

8. 

lose

____

__________ key.

9. 

miss

____

____

2. ‚Past participle '-Formen

Es ist etwas passiert, und du interessierst dich für das **Ergebnis** oder die **Folgen,** (nicht dafür, wann es passiert ist). → Du brauchst das *present perfect.* → So wird das *present perfect* gebildet:

	has/have	+ *past participle*
He/She/It	*has*	*seen* a ghost.
I/You/We/They	*have*	*missed* the bus.

Es gibt zwei Arten von *past participle* →

Regelmäßige	**Unregelmäßige**
Grundform + *-ed*	(Grundform)
kick*ed*	eaten (eat)
jump*ed*	cut (cut)
miss*ed*	lost (lose)

Wie heißen die Grundformen dieser unregelmäßigen *past participles*?

done – ______, had – __________, left – __________, seen – ________, went – ______,

Wenn du Schwierigkeiten mit diesen unregelmäßigen Formen hast, lerne sie am besten auswendig.

3. Can you tell these jokes in English?

1. Doctor, Doctor, I've eaten a pencil.
2. Man in Florida: I've come here for the winter.
3. Woman in cafe: Waiter, what kind of soup is this?
   Waiter: It's bean soup.

a) I don't want to know what it's been. What is it NOW?

b) Then use a biro.

c) Well, you've come to the wrong place. There's no winter here.

have

He has *just* had a shower.

just – gerade eben

She has	*just*	washed her hair.
They have		been shopping.

1.

paint

____

____

2.

clean

____

____

3.

be

____

__________ a football match.

4.

leave

____

____

5.

write

____

__________ some postcards.

6.

make

____

____

7.

buy

____

____

I've just bought a Japanese radio.
– But can you speak Japanese?

These eggs have just come from the country.
– Which country?

1. Some have, some haven't ...

Dave is from Edinburgh. He has just left school and works for a computer firm.

Likes: computer games, listening to rock music, reading detective stories, watching TV, travelling, meeting people from other countries, Italian food, riding his moped.

Kamara and Halim live in Bombay.

Halim has learned to read and write, but Kamara has never been to school. She gets up at four to get water. Then they both help their mother.

Dave *has been* to school.
Kamara *has not been* to school (not - be).
Kamara and Halim *have not learned* German (not - learn).

I/You/We/They He	**have not** **haven't**	**learned** to read.
She/He/It	**has not** **hasn't**	

1. Halim ______________ any computer games (not – play).
2. Kamara ______________ to rock music (not – listen).
3. Halim ______________ any detective stories (not – read).
4. Kamara and Halim ______________ (not – travel). They ______________ people from other countries (not – meet). They ______________ Italian food (not – eat).
5. Kamara ______________ to read and write (not – learn).

2. They have never ...

What do you think? Kamara **has never** ... (seen, had, used ...).
Kamara and Halim **have never** ... (seen, had, used ...).

1. Kamara and Halim have never read a book (read).
2. They ______________ TV (watch).
3. Kamara ______________ to school (be).
4. They ______________ a holiday (have).
5. Halim ______________ a bike (ride).
6. Dave ______________ at four in the morning (get up).

never - nie

And you? I've **never** ...

1. Life in India and Britain

Kamara and Halim live in India, Dave lives in Britain.

already – schon
not yet – noch nicht

It's six o'clock and Kamara *has* **already** *made* a fire. **6.00** Dave *hasn't got up* **yet.**

They have *already* got up.
He hasn't got up *yet*.

Kamara and Halim ____________ ____________ breakfast (have). **7.30** Dave ____________ breakfast ________ (finish).

Halim ____________ to market (go). **8.30** Dave ____________ at work ________ (arrive).

Halim ____________ the shopping (do). **17.00** Dave ____________ the shopping ________ (do).

Halim and Kamara ____________ ________ (eat). **18.00** Dave ____________ his tea ________ (have).

Halim and Kamara ____________ ________ to bed (go). **23.00** Dave ____________ to bed ________ (go).

2. And you? What about today?

I haven't ... *yet.*

I've *already* ...

watched TV
listened to music
had lunch, tea
used a computer
had a hot drink
read a book, comic
played a game
ridden my bike
seen my best friend
...

1. It's ten to six

Remember Dave, Kamara and Halim. Think of a time and ask your partner four questions like this:

It's (ten to six). *Has* Dave *got up yet*?

First you ask a question, then your partner:

It's ... Has/Have ...... yet?
– No, not yet.
– Yes, (he) has / they have.

> So fragst du, ob etwas schon passiert ist oder nicht:
> *Has* Dave *got up* **yet**?
> *Have* Kamara and Halim *got up* **yet**?
> *– No, not yet.*
> – Yes, he has/they have.

Go on:

1. It's half past seven. ________ Halim ________ to market ______ (go)? – ______________________

2. It's a quarter to eight. ________ Kamara and Halim ________ breakfast ______ (have)? – ______________________

3. It's twenty past eight. ________ Dave ____________ at work ______ (arrive)? – ______________________

4. It's half past four. ________ Dave ________ the shopping ______ (do)? – ______________________

5. It's five o'clock. ________ Halim and Kamara __________ ______ (eat)? – ______________________

6. It's a quarter past eleven. ________ Halim and Kamara ________ to bed ______ (go)? – ______________________

Mother: Tommy, have you given the goldfish fresh water yet?
Tommy: No, they haven't finished the old water.

1. Have you ever ...?

ever – jemals

Have you ever seen an elephant?

Yes, in a zoo. Have you?

No, never

Write down eight questions to ask your partner:

Have you ever ...?

been to a pop concert/camping/...?
made a model ship/cake/...?
broken an arm or a leg?
had an accident?
swum in the sea?
played ...?
heard/sung an English song?
seen an English magazine?
got up at four o'clock?
gone to bed after twelve?
used ...?
won anything?
eaten ...?

Have you *ever* eaten spaghetti?
– Yes, lots of times.

1. Have ______________________ ?
2. ______________________ ?
3. ______________________ ?
4. ______________________ ?
5. ______________________ ?
6. ______________________ ?
7. ______________________ ?
8. ______________________ ?

Now ask your partner one of your questions.

Answers:	Yes, lots of times/them.	Yes, once.
	Yes, a few (times).	No, never.

2. Never

Write down three things your partner has never done; for example: Axel *has never ...*

1. ______________________
2. ______________________
3. ______________________

1. I haven't washed my face for a week/since Christmas

Write the beginning of a sentence on a piece of paper.

Start with *I haven't.* They can be funny sentences.

Example:

I haven't been on TV

been to New York
talked to the Queen
bought a Rolls Royce
eaten anything/caviar
listened to the teacher
washed my hands
cleaned my teeth
drunk whisky
visited the President
sung on the radio
made a record
done any homework
learned anything

Fold the paper so you can't see your sentence:

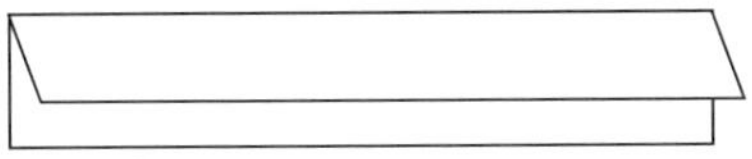

Give your paper to your partner.
Don't read the sentence.
Now write the end of a sentence.
Start with *for* or *since*:

Examples:

for five months | since Christmas

Um zu sagen, dass etwas seit einer gewissen Zeit passiert oder nicht passiert, brauchst du *present perfect* + *for* oder *since*.

I *haven't washed* my face **for** a week.

(eine Woche lang – **Zeitraum**)

I *haven't washed* my face **since** Monday.

(seit Montag – **Zeitpunkt**)

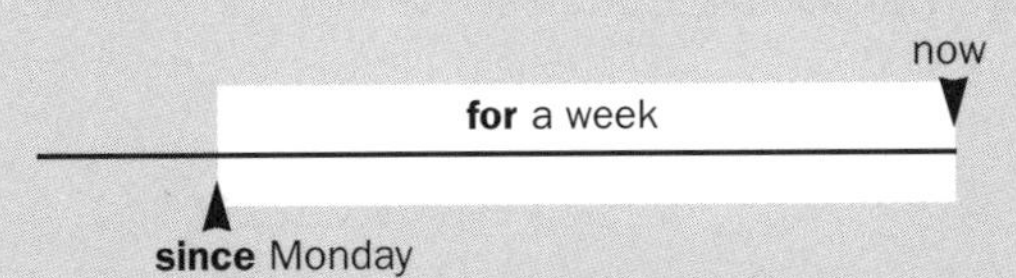

2. Holidays

Herr and Frau Adler are on holiday in Scotland. They are staying at Mrs McCraig's hotel. Mrs McCraig is interested in her German visitors.

For or *since*?

Mrs McCraig: How long have you been in Scotland?

Herr Adler: __________ two weeks.

Frau Adler: We've been in Scotland __________ the middle of July.
But before that we were in England.

Herr Adler: Yes, we've been in Britain __________ the beginning of July.

Mrs McCraig: What! You've been here

__________ so long! Then you must like it.

Frau Adler: Oh yes. We love it.

3. „seit“

Übersetze ins Deutsche.

1. I've had my bike since May. ____________________
2. Peter has been here for a year. ____________________

Unterstreiche die Zeiten in allen vier Sätzen. Was fällt dir auf?

„seit“ + ☐ Präsens
☐ Vergangenheit

for, since + ☐ *present tense*
☐ *present perfect*

Wenn auch im Deutschen *„seit“* im Präsens steht, im Englischen **nur present perfect** geht.

4. A joke

Use *for* or *since* to finish this joke.

Farmer: These are the best eggs we've had ________ years.

Woman: Then please give me some you haven't had ________ so long.

1. Headlines

Do you understand these newspaper headlines?

1. POP STAR BUYS CASTLE FOR CHILDREN'S HOME
2. Chinaman breaks world record
3. GIRL WINS TRIP TO AUSTRALIA
4. Accident in Central London
5. HELPERS PUSH WHALES BACK INTO SEA
6. Woman walks across America – on one leg

What do these headlines mean? Use the *present perfect* of the verbs in brackets to explain.

1. A pop star __________ a castle for a __________ (buy).
2. A Ch __________ the w __________ (break).
3. A __________ a __________ (win).
4. There __________ an __________ (be).
5. __________ some whales __________ (push).
6. A __________ (walk).

> Berichte, Erzählungen oder Gespräche werden im Englischen häufig im *present perfect* ohne Zeitangabe eingeleitet. Die anschließenden Einzelheiten werden jedoch im *simple past* wiedergegeben.

Geht es um das Wann? Wo? Wie? – steht das *present perfect* nie!

2. Details

Can you explain the *details* of the stories? (*simple past*)

a) At seven o'clock last night Maria Gomez __________ in San Francisco (arrive).

b) Last Sunday about a hundred people __________ to push some whales back into the Pacific (help).

c) Last night Li Peng __________ the world discus record (break).

d) A pop star __________ a castle in Romania last week (buy).

e) Last night five people __________ in an accident (die).

f) Fourteen-year-old Jennifer Bailey __________ the happiest girl in her school yesterday (be).

Which story goes with which headline? 1. ____ 2. ____ 3. ____ 4. ____ 5. ____ 6. ____

3. Writing newspaper articles

You are a journalist, working for a British newspaper. Here are the headlines and some notes for your next articles. Write the first two sentences of the articles.

Headline	Article
QUEEN ARRIVES IN GERMANY	The Queen *has arrived* in Germany.
(last Tuesday)	She *arrived* last Tuesday.
1. MANCHESTER UNITED WINS FOOTBALL CUP	M.U. ______________________ (win).
(last night, Wembley)	They __________ at ______________ (win).
2. ACTOR DIES	The actor Robin O'Neil ______________ (die).
(accident, Edinburgh)	He _____ in an __________ in Edinburgh (die).
3. GIRL WRITES BESTSELLER	Eighteen-year-old Sandra Wilmot ______________
(3 months)	a bestseller (write). She ______________ (write)
	it in ______________________ .

4. Translate these sentences

1. Peter hat seine Hausaufgaben gestern nicht gemacht.

   ____

2. Peter hat seine Hausaufgaben noch nicht gemacht.

   ____

3. Ich bin noch nicht in Großbritannien gewesen.

   ____

4. Ich bin letztes Jahr nicht nach Großbritannien gegangen.

   ____

Which German words told you that you needed the *simple past* and not the *present perfect*? Underline them.

Look at these sentences. Which sentence tells us that the Queen's visit is over?

a) The Queen *hasn't met* the German Chancellor yet.
b) The Queen *didn't meet* the German Chancellor.

5. I've done it - I did it yesterday

I've **been** to Italy

Me, too. I **went** two years ago.

1. Why are you here?

Pauline Dent works for a London tourist office. She wants to find out why people visit London. She has given this questionnaire to a group of German schoolchildren, who are visiting London.

1. Why have you come to London? For a holiday ☐ to work ☐ to visit someone ☐
2. How did you get here? By air ☐ By car ☐ By train ☐ By coach ☐
3. Have you been here before? Yes, in/last __________ No ☐
4. Why did you come before? For a holiday ☐ to work ☐ to visit someone ☐
5. How long have you been here? For about __________ days/weeks.
6. When did you arrive? On ________________
7. What have you seen so far?
   Buckingham Palace ☐ The Houses of Parliament ☐ Tower Bridge ☐
   The Tower of London ☐ Saint Paul's Cathedral ☐ Trafalgar Square ☐
   Piccadilly Circus ☐
8. What did you like best? ______________________________

2. Questions

Write the questions down in these lists:

Questions in the ***present perfect***	**Questions in the** ***simple past***
____________________	____________________
____________________	____________________
____________________	____________________
____________________	____________________
Bei diesen Fragen interessieren wir uns **eher für** die ☐ a) Gegenwart ☐ b) Vergangenheit	Bei diesen Fragen interessieren wir uns **eher für** die ☐ a) Gegenwart ☐ b) Vergangenheit

3. Make your own questionnaire

Make up a questionnaire for someone visiting your country.
Can you find someone and ask them?

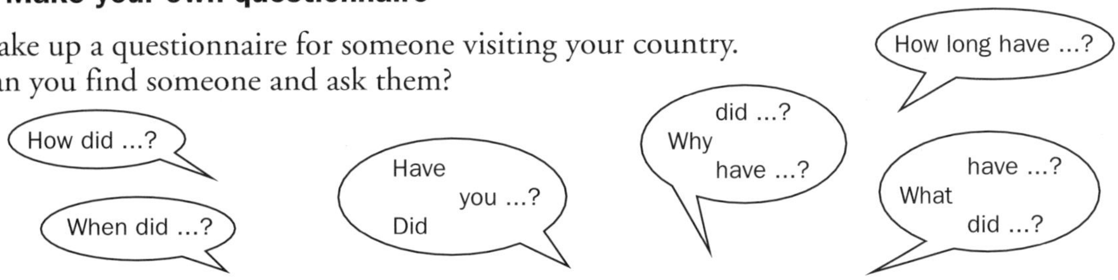

A 32 *Some, any:* Aussagen; Verneinung

1. Our classroom

Can you talk about your classroom in English?
There's **a** blackboard. There **are some** desks. There…

some – einige

2. Yesterday Johnny went shopping

Can you say what he bought?

some – etwas

He bought **some** ...
Some ... And some ...

This was Johnny's shopping list.
Did he get everything?

1 lb. apples
1/2 lb. cheese
coke
biscuits
2 packets of tea
sweets
bottle of milk
cake
bread
jam
yoghurt
coffee

He did**n't** buy **any** ... – kein, keine

Write seven sentences like this:

He bought *some* ______________ , but he

did*n't* buy *any* ________________ .

3. Could you go shopping in Britain?

a can of	orange juice
a loaf of	milk
a carton of	cake
a bottle of	chocolate
a packet of	bread
half a pound of	beans
a jar of	biscuits
a bar of	apricots
two pieces of	jam
a tin of	cheese

A shopping game

You: I went shopping and I bought two tins of apricots.
The next person:
I bought two tins of apricots *and a loaf of bread.*

1. Asking for help

Paul and his friends do their homework together.
Somebody always needs help. Today Paul is having problems with his history homework. He asks, "Can *somebody* help me, please?"
What help do the others need? Use *some – somebody – something*

1. Andy isn't very good at geography.

   He asks, "Can ________________ lend me an atlas, please?"

2. Carol has no ruler.

   She asks, " __________________________________ a ruler, ___________ ?"

3. Diane has no biro.

   She asks, "Can I borrow _______________ to write with, __________ ?"

4. Mike has no paper.

   He asks, "Can ______________ give me __________ paper, please?"

5. Hassan is thirsty.

   He asks, " _____________ have __________________ drink, please?"

6. Lisa is hungry.

   She asks, " ________________________________ to ________ , please?"

7. Mary has forgotten her felt-tips.

   She asks, " ____ felt-tips, __________ ?"

8. Alison has finished her homework first.

   She asks, " ________ I listen to _________ of your CDs, _________ ?"

Can **somebody** help me, please? Can I have **something** to drink? Can you give me **some** paper, please?	*Some (-thing, -body,)* in Fragesätzen, mit denen wir um etwas *bitten* und *'ja'* als *Antwort erwarten.*

2. Politeness

Translate these questions into German.

1. Darf ich dir etwas zu trinken anbieten? Can I get you ____________________________
2. Möchtest du etwas Schokolade? Would you like ____________________________
3. Soll ich dir etwas Interessantes erzählen? Shall I tell you ____________________________

Some (-thing) in Fragesätzen, mit denen wir etwas anbieten wollen.

1. My ideal room

Draw your ideal room – your own room or a classroom. Don't show your picture to your partner.
If you can't draw something, write the English word for it.
But write it where it should be in the room.

Ask your partner about his or her picture. Find out what is in it and try to draw the room:

Is there a ...
Are there *any* ...?
Is there *anybody* in it?

Now look at your drawing and your partner's. Is your drawing like your partner's room?

Are there **any** animals?
Is there **anybody** in the room?
Is there **anything** to eat?

Any (-body, thing) in Fragen, wenn wir die Antwort nicht wissen.

2. Is there anything on tonight?

Can you understand an English TV programme?
Ask your partner questions 1-5, then your partner asks you.

1. You: Is there anything on tonight?
   – Yes, there's ... (at ...).
   – No, not really.
2. Are there any (films/pop programmes)on?
3. Is there anything about (animals/Britain)?
4. Are there any (horror films/detective stories) on?
5. Are there any (sports programmes/comedies) on?

BBC 1

6.00	**Top of the Pops**
6.30	**Wild Life**
7.00	**Comedy:** Carry on
7.30	**Film:** House of Horrors
8.30	**Football:** Milk Cup
9.00	**Documentary:** Scotland
9.30	**Sherlock Holmes:** The Sign of Four
10.30	**Sports News**
11.00	**Film:** Casablanca

1. Danger! Help!

Today many animals, birds and plants are in danger. Look at this Chinese panda. Isn't it nice? But there aren't many pandas now because they only eat bamboo. And there aren't many bamboo forests left.

Did you know?
Many animals are in danger because people kill them for food, clothes and decoration.

2. Why are these animals in danger?

many – viele
not many – nicht viele
not much – nicht viel

Use *there isn't much* or *aren't many* to explain.

Many fish are in danger because there ______________ clean ______________.

There aren't __________ pandas because ______________________ food for them.

Th ______________________ gazelles in Africa because ______________________ grass left.

______________________ elephants because ______________________ forests left.

3. Not many forests, but lots of roads

Use these words to talk about our world: *many, much, a lot of, lots of*

1. There aren't ______________________________________
2. There aren't ______________________________________
3. There isn't ______________________________________
4. There isn't ______________________________________
5. There isn't ______________________________________
6. There are ______________________________________
7. There is ______________________________________

fields forests
land for animals
land for children to play
clean water to swim in
roads houses traffic

Can I do anything to help? – Why not join an organisation?

There **are** many/a lot of/lots of roads. There *is a lot of* traffic.

4. What do you know about deserts?

Write down at least two sentences. Use *There aren't many/isn't much.*

1. How much do you know about the world?

How much? – wie viel?

How many? – wie viele?

Ask your partner all these questions and write the answers down. Then your partner asks you. Check the answers with the teacher at the end.

1. How many people live in your country? About ____________________
2. How many people live on the earth? About ____________________
3. How many continents are there? Can you name them? ____________________

____

4. How many oceans are there? Can you name them? ____________________

____

5. How much of the earth is under water? Lots or only a little? ____________________
6. How much of the earth is under the Pacific Ocean? Lots or only a little? ____________________

____

7. How much of the earth is desert? Lots or only a little? ____________________

How many questions did you get right? ☐ lots ☐ only a few

How many? – **Only a few** (wenige) **Not many**	**How much?** – **Only a little** (wenig) **Not much**

2. What do you think?

1. How many kinds of animals, birds and plants disappear from the earth every year?

   Lots or only a few? ____________________

   ____

2. How many elephants are killed every year? Lots or only a few?

   ____

3. How many kinds of fish are there in Europe's rivers? Lots or only a few?

   ____

3. Test your general knowledge

Tick (✔) the correct answer.

1a) The United Kingdom has more people than Germany. ☐
 b) The United Kingdom has fewer people than Germany. ☐
2a) The USA has more than 40 states. ☐
 b) The USA has fewer than 40 states. ☐
3a) One mile is more than one kilometre. ☐
 b) One mile is less than one kilometre. ☐

fewer than – not as *many* (nicht so *viele*)
less than – not so *much* (nicht so *viel*)

1. Me and my friend

tall, short, old, young, good at ...

I'm tall**er than** my friend.
My friend is ......*er than* me.
My hair's ......*er than* my friend's.

good – *better than*

kurze Adjektive	
tall*er* short*er* old*er*	*than* (als)

2. Compare these things

Use adjectives + ...-*er* and *not as ... as.*

big + *g* + *-er: bigger*
hot + *t* + *-er: hotter*

Example:

a) London – Manchester (big)
London is *bigger than* Manchester.
Manchester is *not as big as* London.

b) The Eiffel Tower – the Empire State Building (high)

The Eiffel Tower is higher than the Empire State Building.

c) India – Sweden (hot)

India is hoter than Sweden

d) Eleven thirty-two – twenty-seven minutes to twelve (early)

early – *-ier: earlier*
easy – *-ier: easier*

e) English – maths (easy)

Maths is easy er than English

f) School on Saturdays – school in the afternoons (bad)

bad – *worse*

School on Saturdays is worse than the school in the afternoons.

3. Can you compare these things?

fast, slow, warm, cold ... (*...-er than* *not as ... as*)

orange juice trains girls going by car February winter

summer boys a year walking water motor bikes

June a month ice-cream camels coffee

Orange juice is better than water. Motor bikes are not as fast as ...

1. Who is the tallest?

Who is the tallest in your class? Who is the shortest?

Now talk about yourself and your family:

tall, short, young, old, long, big, loud, nice, best, worst ...

My ... is the ...*est* in our family.
has the ...*est* (hair/feet/voice ...).
is the *best/worst* at (sports/drawing ...).
is the *best/worst* (swimmer/runner/singer).

good	–	*the best*
bad	–	*the worst*

the	old*est* bi*ggest* ho*ttest* nic*est*

2. How much do you know?

What could you tell a tourist about your country?
(the biggest city? the longest river? the nicest places?)

What do you know about these places? Use the *-est.*

1. Death Valley is ______________ place in the world.
2. Siberia is one of ______________ places in the world.
3. Mexico City is one of ______________ places in the world.
4. The Himalayas are ______________ mountains in the world.
5. The Nile is ______________ river in the world.
6. The cheetah is ______________ animal in the world.

3. Do you know?

-er than, the -est?

1. *high:* Eiffel Tower - tower of Pisa - Empire State Building

   The Eiffel Tower is ______________ the tower of Pisa.

   The Empire State Building is ______________ .

2. *old:* Sphinx – Parthenon – White House

   The Sphinx is ______________ The Parthenon is ______________ the White House.

3. *good, bad*

   Steve is ______________ Peter at maths.

   But Peter is ______________ Steve at English.

   Ann is ______________ at maths. But she is

   ______________ Peter at English. Peter is

   ______________ at maths.

	Maths	English
Steve	42%	37%
Peter	29%	75%
Ann	60%	55%

1. Places

Bonn

exciting
dangerous
beautiful
modern
international
important
expensive

New York

What do you think about these two cities?

... is more interesting than ...

Compare some other places (London, Berlin, my village ...)

längere Adjektive		
more	interesting exciting modern	*than*

1. ______________ is more ______________ than ______________
2. ____
3. ____

2. What's more difficult?

What's more difficult, skiing or skating?

Skiing, I think.

I think skating's just as difficult as skiing.

Ask your partner questions like this. First you ask all the questions, then your partner asks you.

What's
- more difficult – standing on your head or speaking English?/geography or history?/...?
- more difficult to eat – spaghetti or a hamburger with ketchup?
- more interesting – buying clothes or buying records?
- more important to you – pop music or sport?
- more important – giving presents to people or helping people?
- more exciting – a circus or a horror film?
- more dangerous – going by car or travelling by plane?
- more popular – tennis or football?

What do you think?

1. ______________ is more ______________ than ______________
2. ____
3. ____

A 40 Steigerung von Adjektiven: *the most; the -est*

1. The most interesting?

What's *the most* interesting place you know?
(… *the most* interesting book you've ever read?)

the most	interesting dangerous beautiful	*place?*

Think of a question like this and write it on a piece of paper. Then ask your classmates.

What's the most interesting/exciting

- thing you've ever seen/done?
- TV programme/film at the moment?
- school subject?/sport?/hobby?
- music you've ever heard?
- film you've ever seen?
- place near you/in your country?

the most dangerous

- sport?/hobby?
- thing you've ever done/seen?

the most difficult

- school subject/sport?
- thing you've ever done/learned?

the most expensive thing you've ever bought?
the most beautiful thing/place/person you've ever seen?
Who's the most popular singer/band/group at the moment?
What's the most important thing in life for you?

Now write something about yourself. Start with *The most …*

1. *The* ______________________________

2. ______________________________

3. ______________________________

2. Let's make some advertisements

Can you write these advertisements? Use the superlative forms (*the -est* or *the most*) of these adjectives: *beautiful, cold, exciting, expensive, fast, great, modern, warm.* You can use the words more than once.

1.

2.

3.

4.

5.

6.

1. Making the world a better place

We have a lot of problems today. There are too many cars.
We need too much water and energy. We use too many plastic things.
What could we do to make the world a better place?

have showers, not baths

We could ...
People could ...

recycle
collect
use ... again
recycled paper
wrap presents in

could – für Vorschläge *(könnte, könnten)*

stop buying things
in plastic boxes
take shopping bags with us

walk to school/work
go by ...
electric cars
share cars
have more buses and trains
towns without cars

60 people could
go in one bus

2. The good old days

Until Pete's grandmother was 24 she lived on a farm. Her family didn't have much money.
She tells Pete: I *could* play in the streets. There weren't any cars then.
I *couldn't* go out with my friends. I had to help on the farm.

What *could* she do? What *couldn't* she do? What do you think?

take the shopping home by car
swim in the rivers
drive a tractor when she was ten
train for a job
play in the fields
go anywhere by car
buy many new clothes
ride a horse when she was eight

And you?
Write about yourself

I could ... when I was about (ten).
I couldn't ... until (I was about .../
a few years, months ago).

could – *konnte(n)/durfte(n)*
couldn't – *konnte(n)/durfte(n) nicht*

buy my own clothes
use a calculator, computer
cassette recorder
do algebra
go on holiday with friends
go to pop concerts
go out with
play chess/the flute/...
video games
ride a bike
speak English
skate
swim
ski
take photos

1. Rosa has to work, but she would like to go to school

Rosa is thirteen. She comes from Brazil. She lives with her parents and ten-year-old brother in a house made of mud. They have no toilet.

This is what they all have to do – and this is what they would like to do.

Mother	– cook, clean, make bread to sell in the market	have enough money to send her children to school
Rosa	– sell her mother's bread	go to school
Father	– work in the fields	work in an office
Brother	– work in the fields	get a job in a city

would like to
möchte(n)

I/you/we/they	**have to** work.	*Have/Has to* drückt die Notwendigkeit aus, etwas tun zu müssen.
He/she/it	**has to work.**	

Write about the family. Use *have/has to, would like to.*

Rosa's mother *h* ________ cook, ________ and ________ to sell in the market. But she *w* ________ have enough ________ ________ to school. Rosa ________ sell ________ ________ . But she ________ go ________ . Rosa's father and brother ________ work ________ . But her father ________ office and her brother ________ ________ .

2. Do you have to ...?

Rosa has to help her mother at home. What about you? Ask your partner:

– Do you have to help at home?
– No. (Not much/not very often/...)
– Yes, I have to ...

cook clean ... look after
baby-sit take ... for a walk
do the washing/cleaning/shopping/
gardening/washing-up
tidy my room
make the beds
hoover the carpet
mow the lawn

Tell the class about your partner:

– (Michael) *doesn't have* to help at home.
– (Susanne) *has to* look after her baby sister.

don't/doesn't have to

Ask your partner:

– What *don't* you *have* to do?

Then tell the class:

– (Andy) *doesn't have to* ...

Do	I/you/we/they	**have to** help?	Yes	I/you/we/they	**do(n't)**
Does	he/she/it		No	he/she/it	**does(n't)**

Have/Has to auch für **Verpflichtungen**

1. You must do this - you mustn't do that!

Sometimes Martin thinks life is very hard.
So many people tell him what to do and what not to do.

His teacher says:
(be late for school/do your homework/eat in class/forget your books/listen to me/work harder)

1. You *must* ______
2. You ______
3. You ______
4. You *mustn't* ______
5. You ______
6. ______

His mother says:
(come home late/eat so many sweets/go to bed earlier/show me your home-work/always tell me where you're going/watch TV all day

1. You *must* ______
2. You ______
3. You ______
4. You *mustn't* ______
5. You ______
6. ______

Must – für **Gebote** und **starke Verpflichtungen.** Wird meist nur von **Autoritätspersonen** gebraucht. (Ansonsten *have to*).

What else does his teacher or his mother say? What do you think?

must: You ______

mustn't: Y ______

mustn't – nicht *dürfen.* Für **Verbote** und **Warnungen**

2. Have to

Translate these sentences. How do you translate „müssen"?

1. Ich *musste* gestern zum Zahnarzt.	*musste*
______ go to the dentist's yesterday.	______
2. Ich *werde* noch einmal hingehen *müssen.*	*werde ... müssen*
______ again.	______
3. Mein Bruder hat noch nie zum Zahnarzt gehen *müssen.*	*hat ... müssen*
______ never ______ go to the dentist's.	______

Für die Vergangenheit und die **Zukunft** brauchen wir ______ (nicht *must*)

A1

Simple present: ‚s'

1. English is international
Ziel dieses ersten Schrittes ist die Übung der 3. Person Singular des *simple present* und die Erkenntnis, dass Englisch als Weltsprache die Verständigung mit Menschen vieler anderen Nationen ermöglicht (vgl. das weiterführende Gespräch am Ende dieser Einheit).
Die abgebildeten Sprechblasen werden mehrmals von verschiedenen Schülern vorgelesen. Auf die Aussprache und Betonung von *Madrid* [mə'drɪd], '*Manchester U'nited, Ber'lin, Jamaica* [dʒə'meɪkə], *'Amazon, Mi'lan, judo* ['dʒu:dəʊ] und *Moscow* ['mɔskəʊ] soll geachtet werden.
In einer anschließenden Partnerarbeit stellen sich die Schüler abwechselnd Fragen zu den abgebildeten Personen:

A: *Who's Frank?*
B: *He works in a hotel in Berlin. Who's Abdul?*
A: *His father drives a bus in Cairo. Who's ...?*
usw.

Bei dieser Übung wird bewusst gemacht, dass bei der 3. Person Singular des *simple present* ein ‚s' an das Vollverb angehängt wird.

Variante 1:
Es werden 10 Kärtchen, für jede der abgebildeten Personen eines, angefertigt. Auf der einen Seite steht der Name, auf der anderen die dazugehörige Beschreibung, evtl. auch mit Skizze.
Die Karten werden an 10 Schüler verteilt. Diese Schüler kommen nach vorne und stellen sich vor: Zuerst wird der Name gezeigt – *I'm Isabella.* Dann wird die Karte umgedreht: *I live in Madrid. I make clothes.* Nun werden alle Karten so gehalten, dass nur die Namen sichtbar sind. Die Klasse versucht, die Personen zu beschreiben. Dabei können die Schüler entweder das Arbeitsblatt als Gedächtnisstütze benutzen oder sich nur auf ihr Gedächtnis verlassen: *Isabella lives in Madrid. She makes clothes.*

Variante 2: (Gedächtnisspiel)
Nachdem die Schüler die Sprechblasen mehrmals vorgelesen haben, wird das Bild zugedeckt. Die Frage *Who's (Abdul)*? wird von der Lehrkraft oder von verschiedenen Schülern gestellt und entweder schriftlich oder mündlich beantwortet. Nach jeder Antwort wird das Bild kurz aufgedeckt, um die Antwort zu prüfen. Dieses Spiel kann im Klassenverband oder in Partnerarbeit durchgeführt werden. Im letzteren Fall stellen sich abwechselnd zwei Schüler die Frage. Das Spiel eignet sich auch für einen Mannschaftswettbewerb.

● Lösungen
Abdul's father drives a bus in Cairo.
Donna sings in a pop group in Jamaica.
Mona comes from Alaska.
Maria has a kiosk in Milan.
Mehmet sells cars in Ankara.
Isabella lives in Madrid. She makes clothes.
Natasha's mother teaches judo in Moscow.
Mike's brother plays for Manchester United.
Carlos lives on a boat. His father catches fish in the Amazon.

2. Now talk or write about your family
Die Schüler sprechen und/oder schreiben 3–5 Sätze über ihre eigenen Verwandten. Das kann entweder im Klassenverband, in Gruppen- oder in Partnerarbeit geschehen.

Variante:
Jeder Schüler schreibt seinen Namen auf sein Blatt. Anschließend werden die Arbeitsblätter eingesammelt, gemischt und so verteilt, dass jeder ein nicht von ihm selbst verfasstes Blatt erhält. Ein Schüler liest die ihm vorliegende Information vor, und die Klasse versucht den Verfasser zu erraten.
Besonders die Ausspracheregeln sollten nochmals ins Gedächtnis gerufen werden:

[z] nach stimmhaften Konsonanten: [b], [d], [g], [l], [m], [n], [v],
z. B. *sings, loves*
und nach Vokalen: z. B. *plays, goes*
[s] nach stimmlosen Konsonanten: [p], [t], [k], [f],
z. B. *works, makes*
[ɪz] nach Zischlauten: [z], [s], [ʃ], [dʒ], [tʃ],
z. B. *teaches, uses, washes,*

Ein kurzes weiterführendes Gespräch kann im Anschluss die Vorteile einer Weltsprache verdeutlichen, z. B.:

L: *Is it a good thing that so many people learn English? What can you do if you learn English?*

Mögliche Antworten: *Go to different countries; talk to people from different countries; get a job there; get to know different ways of life; get different ideas; learn, think about new things/see things differently/...*

A2

Simple present: don't, doesn't

Your Letters
Als Einstieg bietet sich ein Vergleich mit der einer *problem page* entsprechenden Seite deutscher Jugendzeitschriften an, z. B.: *You all know the German magazine ('Bravo'...), don't you? There's someone you can write to about your problems, isn't there? Like in this English magazine for young people. They can write to Alison. Let's look at some of the letters.*
Die Briefauszüge können entweder von der Lehrkraft oder von einzelnen Schülern vorgelesen werden.
Vor Übungsbeginn ist es hilfreich, auf die zwei Strukturen im Merkkasten hinzuweisen. Die Schüler können für jede Struktur weitere Beispiele aus den Briefen heraussuchen (Partnerarbeit):

– *don't:*
They don't help with the cleaning (Barbara); My parents don't like my hair (Barry); My parents don't know my friends, but they don't like them (John); My friend's hair looks awful. But I don't want to tell her (Maria).

– *doesn't:*
My little brother doesn't have any hobbies (Tony); My sister doesn't eat fruit and she doesn't do sports (Sue); My friend uses my things, but she doesn't ask me first (Helen); My friend doesn't listen to me (Jenny); My sister doesn't feed our hamster. And she doesn't clean its cage (Frank); My friend doesn't bring my comics back (Steve).

1. Who has a problem with …?
In Partner- oder Gruppenarbeit werden die Briefe den drei Kategorien zugeordnet. Man kann die Tabelle auch an die Tafel schreiben und mit den Namen der zehn Jugendlichen beschriebene Kärtchen mittels Klebestreifen in die richtige Spalte heften.

2. What are their problems?
Anschließend werden die Fragen im Klassenverband oder in Einzelarbeit schriftlich oder mündlich beantwortet.

● Lösungen
Brothers or sisters:
Barbara's brothers don't help with the cleaning at home.
Tony's little brother doesn't have any hobbies.
Sue's sister doesn't eat fruit and she doesn't do sports.
Frank's sister doesn't feed the hamster. And she doesn't clean its cage.

Parents:
Barry's parents don't like his hair.
John's parents don't know his friends. But they don't like them.

Friends:
Helen's friend uses her things. But she doesn't ask her/Helen first.
Jenny's friend doesn't listen to her.
Steve's friend takes his comics. But he doesn't bring/take them back.
Maria's friend's hair looks awful. But Maria doesn't want to tell her.

3. And you? Have you any problems with people?
In Partner- oder Gruppenarbeit schreiben die Schüler zwei bis drei ähnliche Probleme bzw. Sorgen auf und lesen sie dann der Klasse vor.

4. Which of these things don't you do? And your friend?
Jeder Schüler stellt eine Liste der Dinge zusammen, die er und auch einer seiner Freunde nicht tut. Dabei soll jeweils dasselbe Verb verwendet werden. Anschließend lesen einzelne Schüler ihre Ergebnisse vor. Zu diesem Zeitpunkt sollte vermieden werden, die Schüler die Struktur *don't/doesn't like* produktiv verwenden zu lassen, um Verwechselungen mit *like …ing* und *like to* auszuschließen.

Variante 1:
Die erstellten schriftlichen Listen werden eingesammelt und gemischt wieder verteilt. Im Klassenverband wird dann spekuliert, wer der jeweilige Verfasser sein könnte. Durch dieses Verfahren lernen sich die Schüler besser kennen.

Variante 2:
Als weitere Übung kann der Lehrer einzelne Schüler dazu auffordern, einen Satz über sich selbst vorzulesen, z. B. *I don't collect stamps.* Der Lehrer gibt vor, schwerhörig zu sein und bittet die Mitschüler um Hilfe: *Sorry, I'm a bit deaf/can't hear very well. She doesn't what?* Die Antwort muss in der 3. Person Singular formuliert werden: *She doesn't collect stamps.*

A 3

Simple present: Aussagen; Verneinung

Animals
In diesem Schritt werden die folgenden vier Strukturen geübt:
*Hamsters **sleep** in the day.*
*Guinea pigs **don't sleep** in the day.*
*The frog **sleeps** in winter.*
*The hedgehog **doesn't sleep** at night.*
Als Einstieg dient das Sammeln persönlicher und allgemeiner Informationen über Tiere, z. B. Haustiere: *Who has a pet? Can you tell us something about (cats)?* Durch mitgebrachte Bilder oder mittels Tafelskizzen wird das Augenmerk auf die in dieser Einheit vorkommenden Tiere gelenkt: *Can you say something about (hamsters, guinea pigs, hedgehogs, frogs, elephants, jaguars, whales)?* Folgende Impulse können an die Tafel geschrieben werden: *come from, live, eat, don't eat, (don't) drink, sleep.*
In einem nächsten Schritt wird der Text auf dem Arbeitsblatt gelesen.

1. Find the right sentences
Anschließend versuchen die Lernenden, in Einzel-, Partner- oder Gruppenarbeit die vorgegebenen Satzelemente einander richtig zuzuordnen und sinnvolle Sätze zu bilden.

● Lösungen
Elephants drink a lot of water.
The Indian elephant doesn't have big ears.
Elephants don't eat meat.
Hamsters sleep in the day.
Guinea pigs don't sleep in the day.
The hedgehog doesn't sleep at night.
The frog sleeps in winter.
The elephant comes from Africa and Asia.
The jaguar lives in South America.
The killer whale doesn't eat people.
Andere mögliche Kombinationen gelten, solange sie sprachlich richtig sind, z. B. *The hedgehog doesn't have big ears.*

Bei schwächeren Schülern kann die Aufgabe dadurch etwas vereinfacht werden, dass nur zwei Spalten einander zugeordnet werden müssen. Die Satzhälften können auch in der Art eines Puzzlespiels auf Papierstreifen geschrieben werden:

Elephants	*don't sleep in the day.*
The Indian elephant	*doesn't eat people.*
Elephants	*drink a lot of water.*
Hamsters	*doesn't have big ears.*
Guinea pigs	*doesn't sleep at night.*
The hedgehog	*comes from Africa and Asia.*
The frog	*sleep in the day.*
The elephant	*don't eat meat.*
The jaguar	*sleeps in winter.*
The killer whale	*lives in South America.*

2. Let's write about some animals
Hier werden die vier Strukturen (vgl. oben *Animals*) zusammen geübt. Der Text kann im Klassenverband, in Einzel- oder Partnerarbeit vervollständigt werden.

● Lösungen
drink – don't drink – doesn't have – eat – don't live – has – doesn't eat – lives – doesn't live – have – don't have

A 4

Simple present: ‚Wh'- Fragen mit ‚do'

1. What do you know about your partner?
Jeder Schüler erhält einen identischen Fragebogen, der in Partnerarbeit ausgefüllt wird. Es ist hilfreich, die Technik des Ausfüllens zu demonstrieren: Ein Fragebogen wird auf den OHP gelegt. Der Lehrer wählt einen Schüler als seinen Partner aus und trägt dessen Namen in den Bogen ein. Dann stellt er diesem Schüler die ersten zwei oder drei Fragen und schreibt die Antworten unter Verwendung der 3. Person Singular auf, z. B.:

1. *plays football, goes for bike rides*
2. *reads adventure stories*

Nach der Lehrerdemonstration wird jede Frage abwechselnd von beiden Schülern in Partnerarbeit gestellt. Die Antworten werden unter Verwendung der 3. Person Singular nur vom jeweils Fragenden eingetragen, z. B.:

1. *plays football, goes for bike rides ...*
2. *reads ...*
3. *watches ...* (Sendung oder Sendungstyp).
   Es sollte darauf hingewiesen werden, dass *programme* mit ‚Sendung' übersetzt wird; (‚Programm' = *channel*).
4. *likes ...*
5. *likes/doesn't like/plays/watches/thinks (football) is ...*
6. *likes/doesn't like/hates/sometimes thinks it's all right/boring ...*
7. *wants to be .../doesn't know yet*
8. *wants to see ...*

2. Exchange sheets
Die ausgefüllten Fragebögen werden so ausgetauscht, dass niemand seinen eigenen Bogen bekommt. Zuerst nimmt der Lehrer einen beliebigen Fragebogen, sucht eine Frage aus und fordert die Klasse auf, zu raten, wie der betreffende Schüler geantwortet haben könnte. Ein Hinweis auf die Strukturen im Merkkästchen unterstützt die Umwandlung in die 3. Person Singular.

L. *I've got Jochen's questionnaire/sheet.*
What books ***does*** *he read? (What do you think?)*

Nach 3–4 Rateversuchen wird die Antwort vorgelesen. Der im ersten Fragebogen vorgestellte Schüler (Jochen) stellt nun seinerseits den ihm vorliegenden Bogen der Klasse mit analogen Fragen vor:

Jochen: *I've got ... 's questionnaire.*
usw.

Variante:
In Gruppenarbeit können die Lernenden versuchen, einen eigenen Fragebogen zu erstellen. Folgende Struktur sollte angegeben werden:
What/Which/Who/How (long/...)/Where/When ***do you ...?***

3. Can you find the joke?

1. *Where do pencils come from?*
2. *Where do snowmen dance?*

A 5

Simple present: always, sometimes, often, never

1. Are horoscopes always right?
Der Lehrer legt den Arbeitsbogen auf den OHP und berichtet, welche Charaktermerkmale ihm in dem vorliegenden Horoskop zugeschrieben werden und wie er darauf reagiert:

L: *Do you ever read horoscopes? Look. This is my horoscope. It's in an English magazine. I'm (Gemini). Look what it says.* (Liest): *"These people never listen to others." That's rubbish. I always listen to other people. And it says: "They are often unhappy". Well, alright, that's true.*

Englische Bezeichnung und Aussprache der Tierkreiszeichen werden wie im folgenden Beispiel durch Vorlesen der Horoskope für einzelne Schüler eingeführt. (Aussprache einiger Tierkreiszeichen: *Pisces* ['paɪsi:z], *Aries* ['eəri:z], *Taurus* ['tɔ:rəs], *Gemini* ['dʒemɪnaɪ], *Virgo* ['vɜ:gəʊ], *Libra* ['li:brə].

L: *My sign's Gemini. That's because my birthday's between May 23 and June 21. It's on June 7.* (Neuerdings zeichnet sich im britischen Englisch die Tendenz ab, wie im amerikanischen Englisch in der Aussprache des Datums den bestimmten Artikel *the* wegzulassen, z. B. *May twenty-third, June twenty-first).*
Who's birthday's from August 23 to September 22?
S1: *Mine – September 6.*
L: *So you're Virgo. Who wants to read S1's horoscope?*
S2: (Liest)
L: *Is that right, S1, or is it rubbish?*
S1: ...
L: *And who's birthday's from ...* usw.

In Gruppenarbeit werden ähnliche und unterschiedliche Charaktermerkmale zusammengestellt. Lernstärkere Gruppen können dies zunächst ohne die Hilfestellung des Arbeitsblattes versuchen. Schwächere vervollständigen die Sätze.

● Lösungen
What's the same?

1. *Aries and Leo people always have fun.*
2. *Pisces and Leo people are never unhappy.*
3. *Aquarian and Leo people are always happy.*
4. *Taurus people often want to know things.*
   And Capricorn people always ask a lot of questions.
5. *Cancer and Capricorn people often think about things.*

What's different?

1. *Pisces people always want to do new things.*
   But Virgo people never want to do anything new.
2. *Pisces people never work very hard.*
   But Aries people sometimes work hard.
3. *Aquarians are never unhappy.*
   But Gemini people are often unhappy.
4. *Gemini people never listen to others.*
   Librans often help others.

2. When's your birthday?
Die auf der Basis des Musterdialogs geführten Gespräche dienen neben dem grammatischen Ziel auch dazu, über den Wahrheitsgehalt von Horoskopen zu sprechen.

What I think about horoscopes
Mündlich oder schriftlich formulieren die Lernenden ihre eigene Meinung zu Horoskopen.

3. Translate these sentences
Das Übersetzen ist hier besonders gut dafür geeignet, den Schülern die unterschiedliche Wortstellung im Deutschen und Englischen bewusst zu machen. Die Regeln werden aus den Beispielsätzen abgeleitet.

● Lösungen
a) Wassermänner haben immer viele Freunde.
b) Fische arbeiten nie sehr viel/hart.

Im **Englischen** stehen *always, sometimes, often, never* **vor** Vollverben wie *have, work*.

Die entsprechenden **deutschen** Wörter stehen dagegen **hinter** dem Vollverb.

Die Suche nach weiteren Beispielen kann in Partnerarbeit erfolgen: *always want (Pisces), sometimes work (Aries), often want (Taurus)*
c) Wassermänner sind immer glücklich.
d) Fische sind nie unglücklich.

Im **Englischen wie im Deutschen** stehen solche Wörter (*always* ...) **hinter** dem Hilfsverb *be*/sein.

Weitere Beispiele: *are sometimes unhappy (Taurus); are often unhappy (Gemini); are never unhappy (Leo).*

A 6

Simple present: Do ...?

1. Do you collect anything?
Die Fragestruktur *Do you ...?* wird anhand eines Fragebogens geübt. Ein Demonstrationsgespräch des Lehrers mit einem Schüler dient zur Einführung unbekannter Wörter und zeigt, wie der Fragebogen ausgefüllt wird. Dazu kann ein Beispiel an die Tafel oder auf den OHP geschrieben werden.
Anschließend werden alle Fragen in Partnerarbeit gestellt und beantwortet: Zuerst stellt Partner A alle Fragen, dann Partner B.
Die beiden Fragen *Do you have brothers or sisters?* und *Do you have a pet?* tragen der wachsenden Tendenz in Großbritannien Rechnung, diese Struktur *Have you (got) ...?* vorzuziehen.

2. Children in other countries
Nachdem in der ersten Übung das *simple present* im Fragesatz nur in der 2. Person Singular geübt wurde, erscheinen nun auch in der 3. Person Plural weitere Subjekte: *all children, they, (more/young) people.* Zuerst wird der die Übung einführende Text gelesen. Bei fortgeschritteneren Lernenden bietet sich ein kurzes Gespräch über die Lebensbedingungen von Schülern in ärmeren Ländern an, wie z. B. der lange Schulweg oder die Schwierigkeit, eine Schule besuchen zu können, weil es an Geld für Kleidung mangelt oder weil die Kinder arbeiten müssen, fehlendes Mobilar, ungenügende Lernmaterialien usw.
In Partnerarbeit übernimmt ein Schüler die Rolle von Joe, der andere stellt Fragen über dessen Leben und Land. Um die Arbeitsweise zu demonstrieren, werden die ersten beiden Minidialoge vom Lehrer und einem Schüler der Klasse vorgeführt:

L: *(S.1), let's say you're Joe. And I want to know something about you and your country.* (Deutet auf die erste Frage: *Do all children go to school?* (Flüstert: *Read the answer*).
S1: *No, some have to work.*
L: *Now let's say I'm Joe. Ask me the next question.* (Deutet auf die nächste Frage auf dem Arbeitsblatt). *Can you do it?*
S1: *Do they all want to go to school?*
L: *Yes, of course. They want to learn to read and write.*

Das Merkkästchen dient als Hilfestellung für die folgende, in Partnerarbeit durchzuführende Frage-Antwort-Übung. Die Verben in der mittleren Spalte erscheinen nicht in der richtigen Reihenfolge und müssen somit von den Schülern sinngemäß umgestellt werden.

● Lösungen
Do you go to school in the afternoons?
Do you do sports?
Do you eat hamburgers or chips?
Do people have telephones?
Do people watch TV in the evenings?

Do people buy things in shops?
Do most people live in towns or villages?
Do most people have cars?
Do young people go to discos?
Do young people live with their parents?

A 7

Simple present: Does ...?/Do ...?

1. Which girl is my sister?
Zunächst wird die Struktur *Does ...?* für sich geübt. Der Lehrer sucht eine der abgebildeten Personen als seine „Schwester" aus, ohne seine Wahl bekanntzugeben. Er fordert die Klasse auf, diese Person zu erraten. Dabei dürfen die Schüler nur drei Fragen stellen und dürfen erst dann einen Namen nennen, wenn sie sich ganz sicher sind, z. B.:

L: *One of these girls is my sister. Can you guess which one? You can only ask three questions like this: Does she ...? For example, Does she collect posters? or Does she play the guitar? You can only say her name when you know who it is.*

Das Ratespiel kann im Klassenverband, z. B. als Mannschaftswettbewerb, oder in Partner- oder Gruppenarbeit durchgeführt werden. Das Spiel kann durch Angabe anderer Namen und Hobbys um beliebig mehr Durchgänge verlängert werden. Es sollten jeweils nur Buben- oder Mädchennamen erscheinen, um die Identifizierung der Person nicht zu leicht zu machen.

2. A quiz
Nachdem die Struktur *Does ...?* isoliert geübt wurde, wird sie jetzt in Verbindung mit *Do ...?* gebracht. Um den Lerneffekt zu optimieren, ist es sinnvoll, die Fragen in Partnerarbeit stellen und beantworten zu lassen. Zuerst stellt Partner A alle seine Fragen. Punkte können für richtige Antworten verteilt werden. Dann stellt Partner B seine Fragen.

● Lösungen
Partner A
1. *homework* = „Hausaufgaben".
2. *I do my homework.*
3. *I live in Germany.*
4. *chips* = „Pommes frites".
5. *Yes, (normally).*
6. *No, (not usually).*
7. *A British person gets Christmas presents on 25 Dec.* (Diese Schreibweise für das Datum setzt sich immer mehr durch. Es wächst auch die Tendenz, wie im AE beim Datum *the* wegzulassen, d.h. *December twenty-fifth*).
8. *In Wales.*
9. *Football.*
10. *No. (He lives at 10 Downing Street.)*

Partner B
1. *TV programme* = „Fernsehsendung" („Fernsehprogramm" = *TV channel*)
2. *How much does it cost?*
3. „ich will" = *I want.*
4. *At nine.*
5. *At (about) four.*
6. *On 25 Dec.*
7. *In Northern Ireland.*
8. *No. 'English' refers to England. 'British' includes England, Scotland, Wales, and Northern Ireland.*
9. *No. (She lives in Buckingham Palace).*
10. *Tennis.*

A 8

Simple present: Who reads ...?/ What do you read?

1. Who has a pet?
Um die unterschiedlichen Formen und Funktionen von Subjekt- und Objektfragen zu erkennen, stellen sich die Schüler gegenseitig Fragen zu ihren Freizeitaktivitäten und tragen die Antworten in eine Tabelle ein. Die Fragetechnik wird mit Hilfe der Tafel oder des Tageslichtprojektors demonstriert. Der Lehrer stellt der gesamten Klasse zuerst die Frage *Who has a pet?* Die Anzahl der Haustiere besitzenden Schüler wird dann in der Spalte *pets* in Form einer Strichliste festgehalten.
Jedem Schüler mit einem Haustier wird nun die Frage gestellt *What kind do you have?* Die Haustierart wird in die Spalte *What kind?* geschrieben. Hinter jeder Haustierart wird durch eine Strichliste ermittelt, wie viele Schüler das jeweilige Tier besitzen.
Bevor sich die Schüler zu der ersten und den restlichen Spalten befragen, lenkt der Lehrer die Aufmerksamkeit auf die Auswahl der Verben oberhalb der Tabelle:
L: *Now, what's next? Animals.* (Deutet auf den linken *substitution table*). *What question do you ask first?*
S: *Who likes animals?*
L: *Yes. And then what do you ask?* (Deutet auf den rechten *substitution table*).
S: *What kind do you like?*
L: *That's right.* (Deutet auf die Spalte *magazines* und den linken *substitution table*). *And what's the first question about magazines?*
S: *Who reads magazines?*
L: *And what's your second question?*
S: *What kind do you read?*
usw.
Auf diese Weise werden alle weiteren Fragen vorbereitet. Sie lauten:
Who watches films? – What kind do you watch?
Who collects things? – What do you collect?
Who likes music? – Which group do you like?
Who goes to a club? – Which club do you go to?
Who plays an instrument? – Which instrument do you play?
In einem nächsten Schritt stellen sich die Schüler ohne Hilfe des Lehrers die Fragen. Die Klasse wird in Dreier- oder Vierergruppen eingeteilt. Turnusmäßig befragt jedes Gruppenmitglied seine Mitschüler zu je einer Spalte mit Hilfe der beiden zu übenden Fragetypen. Jedes Gruppenmitglied trägt die jeweilige Antworten in seine Tabelle ein, z.B.:
S1: *Who has a pet? – What kind do you have, (Sabine)? What kind do you have (Dirk)?* usw.
S2: *Who likes animals? – What kind ...?* usw.

2. Can you remember your questions?
Die Bewusstmachung der unterschiedlichen Fragestrukturen wird durch die Vervollständigung der beiden Listen unterstützt:

animals:	*Who likes animals?*	*What kind do you like?*
collect:	*Who collects things?*	*What do you collect?*
club:	*Who goes to a club?*	*Which club do you go to?*

3. Who likes Pedro?
Die zwei Fragetypen *Who likes ...?* und *Who does ... like?* werden geübt. Die Lösungen sind in Einzel-, Partner- oder Gruppenarbeit zu finden. Die Schüler müssen zunächst die Fragen beantworten und dann in einem neuen Schritt selber die richtigen Fragen finden.

● Lösungen
1. *Pedro*
2. *Barry*
3. *Angela*
4. *Carol*
5. *Who likes Carol?*
6. *Who does Carol like?*
7. *Who likes Hassan?*
8. *Who does Hassan like?*
9. *Who likes Jackie?*
10. *Who does Jackie like?*

A 9

Present continuous: gegenwärtiger Ablauf; Aussagen

Der Verwendung des *present continuous* zum Ausdruck einer noch im Verlauf befindlichen Handlung wird verdeutlicht, indem die gleichzeitigen Tätigkeiten verschiedener Menschen in verschiedenen Ländern beschrieben werden. Durch die Zeitverschiebungen sind alle Personen im selben Moment mit verschiedenen Tätigkeiten beschäftigt.

1. What's the time?
Als Einstieg eignet sich der Hinweis auf die weite Verbreitung der englischen Sprache, unterstützt durch eine Weltkarte:

L: *We're all learning English because people all over the world speak English. For example, in England, in …?* (Schülervorschläge.)

Neben den Schülervorschlägen werden die Länder erwähnt, die auf dem Arbeitsblatt erscheinen: *Turkey, India, Japan, America.* Der Lehrer macht auf die Zeitunterschiede aufmerksam *(What time is it here now? Do you know what time it is in England/Turkey/…?)*
Die Bilder auf dem Arbeitsblatt werden im Klassenverband beschrieben. Dabei sollte die Frage *What is/are … doing?* vermieden werden, um nicht die falsche Antwort **They are doing working* zu provozieren:

L: *Look, when it's eight o'clock in Stuttgart it's nine in Ankara. It's twelve in Delhi. It's four in the afternoon in …* usw. *In Stuttgart Annette's just getting up. In Ankara it's nine. Kemal and Nuray are working. In Delhi it's twelve. Hassan and Ali …?*
S: *Are having lunch.*

Bevor die weiteren Sätze vervollständigt werden, wird die Aufmerksamkeit auf das Merkkästchen gelenkt.
Die Übungen 1, 2 und 3 können mündlich oder schriftlich, in Einzel- oder Partnerarbeit durchgeführt werden.

● Lösungen
1. *It is 8.00 in Stuttgart.*
a) *Hassan and Ali are having lunch.*
b) *In Tokyo it is 16.00. Mr Chang is going home.*
c) *In San Francisco it is 23.00. Mrs Webb is going to bed.*

2. *It is 12.00 in Stuttgart. Annette is shopping.*
a) *In Ankara it is 13.00. Kemal and Nuray are having lunch.*
b) *In Delhi it is 16.00. Hassan and Ali are going home.*
c) *In Tokyo it is 20.00. Mr Chang is watching TV.*

3. *It is 5.00 in Stuttgart.*
a) *In Ankara it is 6.00. Kemal and Nuray are getting up.*
b) *In Delhi it is 9.00. Hassan and Ali are going to work.*
c) *In Tokyo it is 13.00. Mr Chang is having lunch.*
d) *In San Francisco it is 20.00. Mrs Webb is reading a book.*

2. And your family? Your friends?
Die Schüler werden gebeten, sich eine Person aus ihrem Verwandten-, Bekannten- oder Freundeskreis bildhaft vorzustellen und zu überlegen, was jene im Moment des Sprechens wohl tun könnten, z. B.:

Just now I think my mother is working in her office.
My …

Die Konstruktion *is probably …ing* sollte nur dann verwendet werden, wenn sie schon eingeführt wurde.
Jeder Schüler schreibt 1–2 Sätze auf und liest sie anschließend der Klasse vor.

A 10

Present continuous: unterbrochene Handlung; Aussagen, Verneinung

Neben der Funktion, gegenwärtige Abläufe auszudrücken (vgl. A 9), wird das *present continuous* auch gebraucht zum Ausdruck von Tätigkeiten, die angefangen haben, noch nicht zu Ende sind, aber nicht unbedingt im Moment des Sprechens ablaufen müssen, z. B. *I'm learning English/ working in a hotel.* Zur Verdeutlichung dieser Funktion in Aussage- und Verneinungssätzen, erklären verschiedene Personen, warum sie sich im englischen Seebad Brighton gerade aufhalten, bzw. welche Tätigkeiten sie dort ausführen.

1. Brighton in summer
Die erste Übung beschränkt sich auf Aussagesätze. Als Einstieg dient eine Landkarte von Großbritannien. Die Schüler werden aufgefordert, alle Orte, die sie schon kennen, zu nennen. Schließlich wird die Stadt Brighton erwähnt:

L: *Look at this map of Brighton. Which places do you know? Come and show us …*
Do you know this place (zeigt auf Brighton)*? It's called Brighton. It's at the seaside/next to the sea, so a lot of people go there on holiday. But not everyone is on holiday. Look* (deutet auf das Arbeitsblatt), *Kevin works for a Brighton newspaper. He wants …*

Die Übung wird mündlich oder schriftlich, im Klassenverband, in Einzel- oder Partnerarbeit durchgeführt.

● Lösungen
Alain is learning English.
Gudrun is staying with her penfriend.
Carol and Pete are visiting friends.
Barbara and Jill are looking for a job/jobs.
Sue and Dave are working in a hotel.
Lisa is taking photos for a magazine.
Chris and Paul are playing in a band.
Trevor is interviewing tourists.
Anschließend wird die Aufmerksamkeit auf die Regel gelenkt.

2. Memory game
Die Verneinung der *present continuous*-Form wird mit einem Gedächtnisspiel geübt. Zunächst spricht der Lehrer in einem Demonstrationsgespräch über die vorübergehenden Tätigkeiten der abgebildeten Personen. Der Notizblock bleibt abgedeckt, und die Aussagen des Lehrers sind teils richtig, teils absichtlich falsch, z.B.:

L: *Listen. Alain's working in a hotel in Brighton. Is that right or wrong?*
S: *Wrong.*
L: *Yes. It's wrong. He's not working in a hotel. He's …?*
S: *Learning English.*

Das Gedächtnisspiel kann im Klassenverband oder in Partnerschaft durchgeführt werden. Im letzteren Fall stellt Partner A die Fragen 1–4 und Partner B die Fragen 5–8. Vor dem Spiel werden die Lernenden auf die verschiedenen Möglichkeiten bei *You/We/They/He/She/It* (s. Merkkästchen) aufmerksam gemacht.

● Lösungen
1. *That's wrong. He's not/he isn't working in a hotel. (He's learning English).*
2. *That's wrong. She's not looking for a job. (She's staying with her penfriend.)*
3. *That's right.*
4. *That's wrong. They're not/They aren't playing in a band. (They're working in a hotel.)*

5. *That's right.*
6. *That's wrong. They're not learning English.*
   (They're playing in a band.)
7. *That's wrong. They're not working in a hotel.*
   (They're looking for a job.)
8. *That's wrong. She's not staying with her penfriend.*
   (She's looking for a job.)

A 11

Present continuous: Fragen (Is/Are ...?; ‚Wh'-Fragen)

1. Let's draw some pictures
Um die Struktur *Is/Are ... -ing?* zu reaktivieren und auch um neuen Wortschatz einzuführen, entwickelt der Lehrer eine Tafel- bzw. Tageslichtprojektorskizze, die eine Tätigkeit darstellt. Er fordert die Schüler auf, diese Tätigkeit zu erraten. Um keine sprachliche Verwirrung zu stiften, sollte die Struktur *What is/are ... doing?* zu diesem Zeitpunkt vermieden werden.

L: *Look, I'm drawing a boy.*
Is he standing or sitting? Let's see.
(Zeichnet weiter)
Is he playing table-tennis maybe?
(Schreibt *Is he ...?* auf)
Or is he talking to someone?
(Zeichnet weiter)
Is he watching a football match?
No. He's reading.

Die Frage *Are ... -ing?* kann durch zwei Figuren dargestellt werden, die die gleiche Tätigkeit ausüben.

L: *Look, I'm drawing Linda and Paul.*
Are they walking? Or ...?
S: *Are they running?*
L: *Well, let's see.*
S: *Are they playing football?*
L: *No.*
S: *Are they playing tennis?*
L: *No.*
S: *Are they playing table-tennis?*
L: *That's right. Look.*

Anschließend entwickeln einzelne Schüler ähnliche Skizze an der Tafel. Mit Hilfe der angegebenen Strukturen versucht die Klasse, die Tätigkeiten zu erraten. Diese Aktivität kann auch als Mannschaftswettbewerb gestaltet werden.

In einem nächsten Schritt zeichnet jeder Schüler auf seinem Arbeitsblatt die abgebildeten Tätigkeiten in beliebiger Reihenfolge in die Kästchen ein. Bei zwei Personen, z.B. *Sue and Andy,* wird nur eine Tätigkeit gezeichnet (beide laufen, schwimmen, singen oder unterhalten sich). Die Schüler dürfen die Bilder ihrer Nachbarn nicht sehen. Partner A versucht, das erste Bild von Partner B zu erraten. Gelingt ihm das mit nur drei Fragen, bekommt er einen Punkt:

Partner A: *Is Linda playing football?*
Partner B: (Auf seinem Bild fährt sie Ski).
No.
Partner A: *Is she reading?*
usw.

Danach versucht Partner B die erste Zeichnung von Partner A zu erraten usw.

2. What are you doing here?
Die Fragestruktur *Wh*-Fragewort + *are you ... -ing?* wird in einem Rollengespräch geübt. Das Demonstrationsgespräch auf dem Arbeitsblatt dient als Vorlage.
Die Fragen können durch das Einsetzen verschiedener Städte oder Länder variiert werden. Entsprechend gibt es verschiedene Antwortmöglichkeiten. Zusätzliche Varianten können an die Tafel geschrieben oder von den Lernenden selbst gefunden werden, z. B.: *camping, hiking, playing in a football match, touring the country, sightseeing, looking for, collecting, making a film, buying (clothes) for my shop, shopping, working in/for ..., training to be a ...*
Fortgeschrittene Schüler können das Gespräch durch weitere Fragen verlängern, z. B. *Do you like it here? When did you arrive? What do you think about the food/...?* Anschließend kann man die Schüler ihre Gespräche der Klasse vortragen lassen, ohne dass sie auf ihre Karten schauen.

Variante:
Der Lehrer stellt zwei zahlenmäßig gleiche Pack Karten her.

Fragekarten

What are you doing here in Milan? *Berlin Australia Turkey* *And where are you staying?*

Antwortkarten

I'm learning Italian. *working visiting ...* *In a hotel/youth hostel/* *With friends/On a camp site/...*

Die Karten werden entweder an die ganze Klasse oder an Gruppen verteilt. In beiden Fällen muss die Zahl der Frage- und Antwortkarten gleich gehalten werden.
Das Demonstrationsgespräch auf dem Arbeitsblatt verdeutlicht die Vorgehensweise: Schüler A stellt mit Hilfe seiner Fragekarte die erste Frage. Schüler B reagiert darauf mit einer Antwortkarte. Schüler A stellt dann die zweite Frage:

A: *What are you doing here in Alaska?*
B: *I'm taking photos for a magazine.*
A: *And where are you staying?*
B: *In a hotel.*

3. What are they doing here?
Die Struktur *Wh*-Fragewort + *he/she/they ... -ing?* wird mittels einer *information gap*-Übung gefestigt. Dabei handelt es sich um einen Übungstyp, in dem gewisse Informationen nur einem Partner zugänglich sind. Im vorliegenden Fall weiß nur ein Partner, warum sich Tony z. B. in Karlsruhe aufhält und wo er übernachtet.
Auch hier ist es hilfreich, die Fragetechnik durch ein Demonstrationsgespräch zu verdeutlichen. Beide Gesprächspartner halten ihre Texte verdeckt. Jeder Partner stellt zwei Fragen zu der Person bzw. zu den Personen, bei dem bzw. bei denen ein Fragezeichen erscheint, z. B.:

L: *What's Tony doing in Karlsruhe?*
S: *He's learning German.*
L: *And where's he staying?*
S: *With his penfriend.*
L: *Now you ask me about Georgio and Anna:*
What are ...?

S: *What are Georgio and Anna doing in Karlsruhe?*
usw.

Wie im obigen Demonstrationsgespräch sollten die Lernenden nicht zu unnatürlichen, vollständigen Sätzen gezwungen werden.
Beide Fragen werden in Partnerarbeit geübt. Nach einem ersten Durchgang können zur weiteren Übung die Rollen von Partner A und Partner B vertauscht werden.

A 12

‚Simple present' und ‚present continuous' im Vergleich

1. American Indians
Als Einstieg werden Informationen über amerikanische Indianer gesammelt. *(What do you know about American Indians?)* Die geographische Lage des Hopi-Reservats lässt sich am besten anhand einer Amerikakarte demonstrieren. (Es befindet sich zusammen mit dem Navaho-Reservat im Staate Colorado, nördlich der Städte Flagstaff und Albuquerque). In Vorbereitung auf die anschließende Übung wird während der Informationssammlung unbekannter Wortschatz eingeführt, z. B.:

Some Indians make beautiful rugs, jewelry, and baskets.
They often sell these things at a tourist center on the reservation.
They often live in caravans (or prefabricated bungalows).

Eine *reading comprehesion*-Aufgabe verlangt von den Schülern, in Partner- oder Gruppenarbeit die abgebildeten Personen so zu benennen und mit ihren Tätigkeiten zu beschreiben, wie im ersten Bild vorgegeben *(Dorothy is making a rug).*

● Lösungen
a) *Sarah is making bread.*
b) *Maria and Susanna are making baskets.*
c) *Mike is making jewelry.*
d) *Ben and Adam are working in the fields/planting corn.*
e) *Anna is riding her motorbike.*

Um den unterschiedlichen Gebrauch von *simple present* und *present continuous* bewusst zu machen, werden die Verben in Dorothys Bericht unterstrichen und daraus Schlüsse auf die Regeln gezogen. Unterstrichene Verben:
make – isn't making – she's making – sell – takes – works – He's making – makes – she's helping – have – are working – They're planting – goes – She's riding
Aus diesen Beispielen werden folgende zwei Regeln erarbeitet:

Wir verwenden das *simple present* für Dinge, die man *üblicherweise/normalerweise/immer tut,*
z. B. *Sarah and I make rugs.*
Wir verwenden das *present continuous* für Dinge, die man *gerade im Moment/jetzt gerade tut bzw. nicht tut,*
z. B. *Sarah isn't making one right now/She's making bread.*

2. Life on the reservation
Die Schüler stellen sich vor, sie unterhalten sich mit den Indianern über das Leben in dem Reservat. In Partnerarbeit vervollständigen sie die Aussagen der Indianer.

● Lösungen
Maria: *I'm helping – make – is making – come – sell*
Mike: *work – sell – I'm making – make – take*
Ben: *work – like*

In einer weiteren Partnerarbeit sammeln die Lernenden Signalwörtern für die in den vorausgegangenen Berichten verwendeten Zeiten.

● Lösungen
simple present: usually, three days a week, always, sometimes, every day
present continuous: today, right now

3. What I know about American Indians
Der Eingangstext soll, etwas verändert, als Lückentext vervollständigt werden, wobei die Schüler ständig zwischen *simple present* und *present continuous* wählen müssen. Schwächere Schüler können den Eingangstext vor der Übung noch einmal durchlesen. Ansonsten sollen sich die Lernenden auf ihr Gedächtnis stützen.
Die Übung kann als Partnerarbeit durchgeführt werden oder als ein Wettbewerb zwischen verschiedenen Gruppen.

● Lösungen
The Hopis live in caravans on a reservation. They make things and sell them at their tourist center. Dorothy and Sarah make rugs, but today Sarah is making bread.
Mike usually works at the tourist centre, but right now he is making jewelry. Maria usually makes bread, but today she is helping (Susanna) to make baskets. The Indians also have fields. Today Ben and Adam are working in the fields. They are planting corn.

What else would you like to know about American Indians?
In einem weiterführenden Projekt werden die Schüler aufgefordert, einige Fragen zu amerikanischen Indianern selbst zu formulieren. Zudem sollen sie weitere Informationen selbständig herauszufinden suchen.
Beispiele für weitere Fragen:
Do they have to live on a reservation?
Are there different reservations for different tribes?
Who owns the reservations/land?
What is a reservation like?
Where do the Indians work? Is there work on the reservation?
What kind of places do they live in? (Houses, caravans, tents?)
Do they still wear traditional clothes/have traditional celebrations?
What do they eat?

A 13

Future: ‚going to' (Schlussfolgerungen)

In dieser Einheit wird *going to* mit der Funktion geübt, aus der Gegenwart Schlussfolgerungen für die Zukunft zu ziehen. Abbildungen dienen zur Kontextualisierung der Struktur und als visuelle Stimuli für die sprachliche Übung.

1. What's going to happen?
Die Sätze werden entweder im Klassenverband, in Einzel- oder Partnerarbeit vervollständigt.

● Lösungen
1. *It's going to rain.*
2. *She is/'s going to fall into the water.*
3. *They are/'re going to drop the sofa.*
4. *Arsenal isn't going to win the football match.*
5. *They are/'re going to miss the bus.*
6. *They're not/aren't going to cross the bridge.*
7. *The factory is/'s going to close.*
8. *She isn't/'s not going to pass the maths exam.*
9. *They are/'re going to break the window.*

Die Regel wird von den Lernenden selbst formuliert: Wir verwenden *going to, wenn wir aus der Gegenwart Schlussfolgerungen für die Zukunft ziehen können.*

A 14

Future: ‚going to' (Absichten, Pläne)

Diese Einheit beschäftigt sich mit *going to* in der Funktion „etwas beabsichtigen, planen".

1. I'm going to ...
In dieser Übung wird die 1. Person Singular geübt. Der Lehrer beginnt mit einem kurzen Bericht darüber, was er heute oder am Wochenende vorhat bzw. nicht vorhat, z. B.:
L: *It's a nice day today. After school I'm going to lie in the sun (do my marking outside/go swimming/...). I'm going to have a busy afternoon/weekend: On Saturday afternoon I'm going to (do lots of marking/visit someone in hospital/take ... to the cinema/...)*

Anschließend befragt der Lehrer einzelne Schüler über deren Pläne für den Nachmittag bzw. das Wochenende. Die Struktur *What are you going to do?* sollte zu diesem Zeitpunkt vermieden werden, um die Schüler nicht unnötig zu verwirren und die falsche Reaktion **I'm going to do play ...*) zu provozieren:
L: *What about you?*
(Flüstert oder deutet auf einen Tafelanschrieb): *I'm going to ...*
S1: *I'm going to ...*
L: *And you, S2?*
S2: *I'm going to ... / I don't know yet.*

2. Are you going to ...?
Der Lehrer stellt fünf bis sechs Schülern die Frage *Are you going to ... this afternoon/weekend? (do sports/visit anyone/see your friends/watch a film/play video games/read a book/do any shopping/...).* Der Musterdialog auf dem Arbeitsblatt gibt die Struktur für die nachfolgenden Partnerinterviews vor.
Die ‚Interviews' werden in Partnerarbeit durchgeführt, wobei die Antworten notiert werden. Anschließend werden die Antworten der Klasse vorgelesen, z. B. *Axel is going to see a friend.*
Die Regel wird zusammen mit den Schülern erarbeitet: Wir haben immer *going to* benutzt, weil es sich um *Absichten/Pläne* handelt.

3. Holiday plans
In Gruppen versuchen die Lernenden, die Urlaubspläne der drei Personen zu versprachlichen. Wortschatzhilfen können angeboten werden: *travel, go by, stay, take photos, have a look at, visit some ...* Die Schüler können aber auch dazu ermutigt werden, nach unbekanntem Wortschatz zu fragen bzw. zu suchen.

● Lösungen
Andy is going to travel/go by train. He is going to stay in hotels. He is going to take photos. He is going to have a look at/visit British cities. He is going to draw (some) pictures. Barbara and Jackie are going to go on (a) bike ride(s)/tour(s). They are going to stay in a caravan (by the sea/on the coast). They are going to swim. They are going to listen to cassettes. They are going to read (books). They are going to write letters.

A 15

Future: ‚will' (unbeeinflussbares Geschehen; Aussagen)

In dieser Einheit wird *will* in der Funktion, ein künftiges Geschehen auszudrücken, das der Sprecher nicht beeinflussen kann, geübt. Diese Funktion wird eingangs durch einen Fragebogen zu Prognosen über die Zukunft verdeutlicht. Bevor die Fragebogen ausgeteilt werden, kann man ein kurzes Gespräch über die Zukunft führen. Dabei lässt sich auch unbekannter Wortschatz einführen:
L: *Have you ever thought about the future, let's say a hundred years from now? Do you think things will be like they are now? Or will things be different? What will life be like?*

Als Hilfestellung und zur Einführung der ersten Übung können einige Wörter an die Tafel geschrieben werden, z. B. *live, work, schools, traffic, life at home, the world, trees, sea.*
Nach einigen Schülerbeiträgen wird der Fragebogen ausgeteilt.

1. 100 years from now
Jeder Schüler unterstreicht in Stillarbeit die zutreffenden Buchstaben. Bei jeder Frage können mehrere Antworten zutreffen. Anschließend werden die Antworten der Klasse vorgetragen.
Beispiel:
L: *Now what about the first question?*
S1: *I think most people will live in flats and in towns.*
S2: *I don't. I think ...*
etc.

Fortgeschrittenere Schüler können die Antworten weiterdiskutieren und eigene Ideen hinzufügen.
Beispiel:
1. – *I think most people will live in towns.*
   – *Why?*
   – *Because there won't be/they won't find enough work in the villages.*
3. – *I think children will have to go to school some times, but not every day.*
   – *I don't. I think they'll learn at home from machines.*
   usw.

4 c). *They'll travel by ... / have private planes / There'll be trains everywhere / They'll go everywhere by ... / ...*
5 c). *... food. They'll eat pills.*

2. Will / won't
Die Regel sollte möglichst von den Lernenden selbst erarbeitet werden, wie etwa, die *,wir nicht beeinflussen können/die geschehen werden, ob wir es wollen/planen oder nicht'.*
Die Aufmerksamkeit sollte auch auf die Interferenzfalle *will* = „werde" und nicht „will" gelenkt werden, sowie auf die Stellung von *probably* vor *won't.*

3. Translate into German
Der unterschiedliche Gebrauch der Tempora im Deutschen und Englischen für die Zukunft wird durch eine Übersetzung verdeutlicht:
In hundert Jahren gibt es wahrscheinlich keine Bäume mehr / wird es wahrscheinlich keine Bäume mehr geben.

4. My ideas about the future
In Einzel-, Gruppen- oder Partnerarbeit schreiben die Lernenden eigene Ideen auf. Schwächere Schüler können auf die vorgegebenen Ideen zurückgreifen, fortgeschrittenere können eigene Gedanken formulieren. Die Lernenden sollten dazu ermutigt werden, unbekannten Wortschatz nachzuschlagen bzw. danach zu fragen.
Vorschläge für weitere Hilfestellungen:
live on the moon, cities
won't go to work/school any more
there won't be any …
robots do all the work
learn from computers at home

5. Can you match these jokes?

● Lösungen
1. b) 2. d) 3. a) 4. c)

A 16

Future: ,will' (spontane Entschlüsse)

In dieser Einheit wird *will* mit der Funktion, einen spontanen Entschluss zum sofortigen oder künftigen Handeln auszudrücken, geübt.

1. How can these people help?
In Einzel- oder Partnerarbeit werden Kurzdialoge vervollständigt.

● Lösungen
I'll carry it for you.
I'll go and ask.
I'll shut the window.
I'll help you.
I'll take you.
I'll get you a drink.
Der Merkkasten stellt den unterschiedlichen Gebrauch der Zeiten im Deutschen und im Englischen heraus.

Wann gebrauchen wir „I'll"?
Die Regel wird zusammen mit den Lernenden erarbeitet:
Wenn wir spontan Hilfe anbieten oder Vorschläge machen.

2. What do you say?
Im Klassenverband, in Partner- oder Gruppenarbeit verbalisiert Schüler A eine der Sprechblasen. Schüler B reagiert mit einer sinngemäß richtigen Äußerung, die er der rechten Seite des Arbeitsblattes entnimmt. Nach jedem Minidialog werden die Rollen getauscht.
Fortgeschrittenere Schüler erhalten nur die Sprechblasen (fotokopiert oder auf einzelnen Kärtchen), passende Reaktionen müssen sie selbst formulieren.

● Lösungen
Can someone check my homework, please? – I'll do it.
I'm late for school. – I'll take you on my bike.
I need some stamps. – I'll get you some when I go out.
I'm hungry. – I'll get you a sandwich.
My anorak's upstairs. – I'll get it for you.
There's been an accident. – I'll phone for an ambulance.
My train arrives at half past six. – I'll meet you at the station.
I'd like a coke. – I'll buy you one.
I've left my exercise-book at home. – I'll give you some paper.
I want to go to town this afternoon. – I'll come with you.
It's hot in here. – I'll open the window.
It's our teacher's birthday on Monday. – I'll make a cake.

A 17

Future: ,will' (unbeeinflussbares Geschehen; Fragen, Kurzantworten)

1. Travelling to Germany
Mit Hilfe einer Landkarte bzw. der Skizze auf dem Arbeitsblatt wird die Situation kurz eingeführt:
L: *You can all speak English, can't you? So some time you'll probably want to go to England. You'll want to have a look at the country and talk to the people. How will you get there? (By …?)*
S1: *By train.*
S2: *Or you can fly.*
L: *And how will you get across the Channel?*
S: *By boat/ferry.*
L: *And then?*
S: *Then by train or by coach.*
L: *That's right. Now look at this map* (Arbeitsblatt). *This is Jean. She's English and she lives in London.* (Liest die Einführung auf dem Arbeitsblatt).

Die ersten Fragen werden vom Lehrer vorgeführt mit einem Hinweis auf die Satzmuster im Merkkästchen. Die weiteren Fragen werden entweder im Klassenverband oder in Partnerarbeit beantwortet.

● Lösungen
Beide Formen *will* und *'ll* werden akzeptiert. Die Kurzform hat den Vorteil, dass sie ein natürlicheres Sprechen begünstigt.
1./2. –
3. *No, they won't. They'll go by boat/ferry/hovercraft.*
4. *No, it won't. It'll/will arrive in the afternoon.*
5. *No, it won't. It'll/will land in Belgium.*
6. *Yes, she will – in Mannheim.*
7. *No, he won't.*
8. *No, she won't. She'll arrive on Sunday.*

2. What are the questions?

● Lösungen
1. –
2. *How will she get to Ramsgate?*
3. *When/What time will she arrive in Ramsgate?*
4. *How long will they be on the boat?*
5. *How will they get to Germany from Ostend?*

A 18

Simple past: regelmäßige, unregelmäßige Formen; Aussagen

1. Using your dictionary
Ein Zeitungsausschnitt mit mehreren u.U. unbekannten unregelmäßigen *simple past*-Formen fordert die Schüler zum Gebrauch eines Wörterbuchs heraus. Ein Wörterbuchausschnitt verdeutlicht diesen Suchgang.
In Partnerarbeit suchen die Schüler im Wörterbuch oder in einer Liste regelmäßiger und unregelmäßiger Verben (meistens im Lehrbuch) nach den Grundformen der angegebenen *simple past*-Formen und versuchen, die Regel zu vervollständigen:
stole – steal, left – leave, ran – run, held – hold, could – can
Bei *simple past*-Formen muss ich die *Grund*formen nachschlagen.
Das Merkkästchen ruft die Funktion des *simple past* in Erinnerung.

2. ‚simple past'-Formen
Die Tabellen können in Partnerarbeit ausgefüllt werden.

● Lösungen
Regelmäßige Verben: *helped, played, wanted, liked, phoned, stopped* (Schreibweise!), *tried* (Schreibweise!).
Der Lehrer sollte neben der auf dem Arbeitsblatt angegebenen Schreibregel für die *simple past*-Form regelmäßiger Verben auf die drei Aussprachevarianten des *past tense*-Morphems achten:
[d] nach stimmhaften Konsonanten und Vokalen: z. B. *opened, played.*
[t] nach stimmlosen Konsonanten: z. B. *walked, liked.*
[ɪd] nach [d] und [t]: z. B. *hated, painted*
Die Schüler sollten weiterhin an folgende Schreibregeln erinnert werden:
- Wenn die Grundform auf *e* endet, wird nur *-d* angehängt *(like, phone).*
- Endkonsonanten werden verdoppelt *(stop, travel).*

Unregelmäßige Verben: *was/were, went, got, made, rode, saw, took.*

3. Indian 'books'
Die erste Geschichte kann vom Lehrer eingeführt und im Klassenverband vervollständigt werden. Alternativ erscheint die Bildgeschichte mit abgedecktem Text auf dem Tageslichtprojektor, und die Schüler versuchen mit Hilfe des Lehrers, z. B. durch Angaben von Verben im Infinitiv, die Geschichte zu verbalisieren.
Die folgenden zwei Geschichten werden in Partner- bzw. Gruppenarbeit ausgefüllt und anschließend vorgelesen.

● Lösungen
1. ... *He could not/couldn't swim. Silver Hand saw Red Foot's pony. He took the pony. He rode the pony next to the river. He found Red Foot. He pulled Red Foot out of the river. They rode home together.*
2. *Black Leg went to the woods to find food. He fell down and broke his leg. He could not/couldn't walk. Big Man saw his bag. He found Black Leg. He gave him something to drink. Then he rode back to the village to get help.*
3. *Brown Bear went to the mountains to look for food. He fell into a hole. He could not/couldn't get out. Little Foot saw Brown Bear's/his pony. He found Brown Bear. He pulled him out of the hole. They rode home together.*

Variante:
Fortgeschrittenere Schüler sollten versuchen, mit Hilfe der Symbole eigene Indianergeschichten zu schreiben. Dazu können auch eigene, zusätzliche Symbole erfunden werden.

And your story?
Mit Hilfe von selbst erfundenen Symbolen versuchen die Lernenden, etwas aus ihrer eigenen Vergangenheit zu erzählen, z. B. was sie am vorigen Tag, Wochenende oder im Urlaub gemacht haben. Partner- oder Gruppenarbeit erleichtert das Erfinden passender Symbole.

A 19

Simple past: Verneinung

In dieser Einheit werden verneinte Sätze mit modalen Hilfsverben und Vollverben im *simple present* geübt.

1. Wanda, the pop star
Der Text über Wanda wird entweder vom Lehrer oder von Schülern vorgelesen. Die anschließende Gegenüberstellung *Ten years ago – Today* kann im Klassenverband oder in Partnerarbeit, mündlich oder schriftlich vervollständigt werden.

● Lösungen
She didn't/couldn't go to parties.
She didn't/couldn't buy many clothes.
She didn't/couldn't travel much.
She didn't know any pop stars.
She didn't/couldn't go on holiday.
She didn't/couldn't stay in hotels.
She couldn't speak German.
She couldn't dance.
She couldn't play any instruments.
She didn't meet many people.
She didn't get many letters.
People weren't interested in her.
She wasn't very fit.
She wasn't very happy.
Die Bildung der Verneinungsformen kann durch einen Hinweis auf die Merkkästen kurz in Erinnerung gebracht werden.

2. And you?
In Partner- oder Gruppenarbeit schreiben die Schüler drei Sätze auf, z. B. *I couldn't speak English. I didn't play (foot-*

ball)/have a computer/come to this school/couldn't play the flute/ski ...
Sie sollten ermutigt werden, nach unbekanntem Wortschatz zu suchen bzw. zu fragen. Anschließend werden die Sätze vorgelesen.

A 20

Simple past: Fragen mit ‚Did ...?'; ‚Was/Were ...?'; Kurzantworten

1. A Health Quiz
Als Einstieg bietet sich an, einige Fragen über den Verlauf des vorigen Tages zu stellen. Dabei sollten Fragen mit Fragewörtern *(What did you do?)* vermieden werden, um keine Verwirrung zu stiften: *Let's see what everyone did yesterday after school. (Annette), did you do any sports yesterday? Did you watch TV? (Jochen), did you ...?* usw. Es wird nur mit *Yes, I did* bzw. *No, I didn't* geantwortet.
Die Fragebogen werden in Partnerarbeit ausgefüllt. Es ist hilfreich, wenn der Lehrer die Technik vorher demonstriert: Der Fragebogen erscheint auf dem OHP. Der Lehrer befragt einen Schüler und kreuzt die entsprechenden Kästchen an.

2. Stop, thief!
Nachdem die Schüler an die *past tense*-Formen von *be* erinnert wurden, versuchen sie, den Dialog zu vervollständigen. Das kann schriftlich oder mündlich erfolgen.

● Lösungen

Were you out for long?	*No, I wasn't. Only an hour.*
Were the windows open?	*No, they weren't.*
Was the chair under the window?	*Yes, it was.*
Were these clothes on the floor?	*Yes, they were.*
Was this knife on the table?	*No, it wasn't.*
Were the wardrobe doors open?	*No, they weren't.*

The thief is in the wardrobe.
Fortgeschrittenere Schüler können den Dialog zu einer kleinen Spielszene erweitern, z. B. indem sie den Dieb im Schrank finden (*Inspector* schaut in den Schrank: *Well now, look here. I think we've found the thief, haven't we! Give me your name.* Ruft nach Polizisten, die draußen stehen usw.)

A 21

Simple past: ‚Wh'-Fragen (What did ...?)

1. Find the jokes
Die Struktur Fragewort + *did* wird zunächst durch eine Zuordnungsübung passiv geübt. Im Klassenverband, in Einzel- oder Partnerarbeit werden die zwei Listen so zusammengefügt, dass folgende Witze entstehen:
1. *What did one ghost say to the other? – Do you believe in people?*
2. *What did Big Chief Running Water call his two sons? – Hot and cold.*
3. *How did you find the weather when you were on holiday? – I just went outside and there it was.*
4. *Why did the pioneers cross America in waggons? – They didn't want to wait 40 years for a train.*
5. *What did one wall say to the other? – Let's meet at the corner.*
6. *How did the accident happen? – A sign said STOP! LOOK! And while I did the bus hit me.*

Die Regel wird von den Schülern erarbeitet:
Fragewort + ***did*** + *Grundform*
What ***did*** *the ghost say?*
When ***did*** *you arrive?*
Where ***did*** *they go?*

2. Did you like London?
Die beiden Dialoghälften werden in Partnerarbeit behandelt. Das Gespräch wird zuerst durch den Lehrer und einen Schüler vorgemacht. Fortgeschrittenere Schüler können die Antworten variieren.
L: *When did you go to London?*
S: *In the summer holidays.*
L: *Where did you stay?*
S: *In a (youth hostel).*
usw.

● Lösungen
2. *Where did you stay?*
3. *How did you get there?*
4. *How long did you stay in London?*
5. *How did you get around?*
6. *What did you see?*
7. *What did you eat?*
8. *What did you do at night?*
9. *How many photos did you take?*
10. *What did you like best?*

Nach dem ersten Durchgang werden die Rollen getauscht, sodass Partner B die Fragen stellt. Die Übung kann durch Reduzierung der Hilfestellungen erschwert werden: Lediglich Stichworte wie *stay, get there, get around, see, eat, do at night, take photos, like best* werden an die Tafel bzw. auf den OHP geschrieben. Sowohl die Fragen als auch die Antworten müssen dann frei formuliert werden. Die Gespräche können danach der ganzen Klasse vorgeführt werden.

3. What were the questions?
Die Regel für die Fragebildung mit *be* wird kurz in Erinnerung gerufen:
How long were you on the boat?
What was it like in London?
Wir brauchen kein *did* beim Verb *be.*

A 22

Simple past: ‚Wh'-Fragen (Who painted ...?/What did he paint ...?)

Die beiden Fragesatztypen *Who painted ...?* und *What did he paint ...?* werden anhand von Quizfragen zur Allgemeinbildung geübt.

1. A quiz
Die Schüler befragen sich in Partnerarbeit: zuerst stellt Partner A Fragen 1–5, dann Partner B Fragen 6–10.
Im Anschluss an die Partnerarbeit werden die Antworten im Klassenverband überprüft.

● Lösungen
1. *Yuri Gagarin* 2. *Leonardo da Vinci* 3. *Sydney* 4. *In 1492* 5. *Detective stories* 6. *A detective (in English books)* 7. *London* 8. *China (A. D. 105)* 9. *Latin* 10. *Tennis*

2. Questions! Questions! Questions!
Um die dem Übungsgeschehen vorausgehende Regel zu erklären, sollte der Begriff „Subjekt" bekannt sein.
Die nachfolgende Übung kann in Einzel- oder Partnerarbeit gemacht werden.

● Lösungen
1. *Who spoke Latin?*
2. *What did the Romans speak?*
3. *Who went to America first?*
4. *When did Columbus go to America first?/he go there first?*
5. *Which famous musician lived in Austria?*
6. *Where did Mozart/he live?*

A 23

Present perfect: Ergebnis, Folgen

1. What has happened?
Die Bilder werden mit Hilfe der angegebenen Verben beschrieben. Das kann im Klassenverband, in Einzel- oder Partnerarbeit, mündlich oder schriftlich erfolgen. Die Schüler sollten dazu angeleitet werden, beim Sprechen die Kurzformen zu gebrauchen.

● Lösungen
1. *He has eaten too much cake.*
2. *She has broken her leg.*
3. *They have kicked the ball through the window.*
4. *She has fallen off her bike.*
5. *He has made a model ship.*
6. *The cat has jumped on(to) the wall.*
7. *He has seen a ghost.*
8. *She has lost her key.*
9. *They have missed the bus.*

2. ‚Past participle'-Formen
Funktion und Bildung des *present perfect* werden in einem Flussdiagramm zusammengefasst. Fortgeschrittenere Schüler können versuchen, zunächst ohne Hilfe des Diagramms die Funktion des *present perfect* aus den vorausgegangenen Sätzen zu erschließen, wie etwa: Wir interessieren uns mehr für das Ergebnis oder die Folgen eines Ereignisses als dafür, wie oder wann es passiert ist.
Den Lernenden sollte klargemacht werden, dass man die *past participles* nicht direkt im Wörterbuch nachschlagen kann, sondern die dazugehörigen Grundformen kennen muss. Die anschließende Bestimmung der Grundformen unregelmäßiger *past participles* kann auf weitere Verben ausgedehnt werden. Es lässt sich auch ein Mannschaftswettbewerb daraus entwickeln.

● Lösungen
do – have – leave – see – go

3. Can you tell these jokes in English?
In Partner- oder Gruppenarbeit werden die Witzhälften einander zugeordnet.
1. b), 2. c), 3. a)

A 24

Present perfect: just

Um die Bedeutung von *just* zu verdeutlichen, mimt der Lehrer einige Handlungen und kommentiert sie anschließend, wie etwa: *I've just washed my hands, hair, feet/had a cup of tea/made a sandwich/written, posted a letter/bought something/...*

Variante:
Der Lehrer holt einen Schüler nach vorne und zeigt ihm einen Zettel, auf dem Anweisungen zu ähnlichen Handlungen stehen, z. B.: *wash your hands/make a cup of tea* usw.
Nachdem der Schüler die Handlung ausgeführt hat, raten seine Klassenkameraden, was er wohl gemacht hat: *He's just ...*
Die Satzstellung von *just* wird durch Beschreiben der Bilder auf dem Arbeitsbogen geübt.

● Lösungen
1. *They have just painted the wall.*
2. *She has just cleaned her bike.*
3. *They have just been to a football match.*
4. *The train has just left.*
5. *They have just written some postcards.*
6. *He has just made a cake.*
7. *She has just bought a plant.*

A 25

Present perfect: Verneinung; ‚never'

1. Some have, some haven't ...
Zunächst werden beide Texte entweder vom Lehrer vorgelesen oder von den Lernenden still gelesen. Die Klasse wird dann aufgefordert, mit Hilfe der angegebenen Strukturen Unterschiede zwischen den drei Jugendlichen aufzuschreiben. Dies kann in Partner- oder Gruppenarbeit erfolgen:

L: *Dave's life is very different from Halim and Kamara's, isn't it? One difference is that he has been to school.* <u>*Kamara hasn't been to school.*</u> *Dave has travelled.* <u>*Halim and Kamara haven't travelled.*</u>

Der Lehrer schreibt die unterstrichenen Sätze an die Tafel bzw. auf den OHP und weist kurz auf die Strukturen im Merkkästchen hin. Folgende Strukturen und Wortschatzangaben sind hilfreich:
Dave has (been, learned ...). Halim/Kamara ***hasn't*** *... (played, watched)*
Halim and Kamara ***haven't*** *... (met, eaten)*

Mögliche Antworten:
Kamara hasn't learned to read and write.
Kamara and Halim haven't played (any) computer games.
They haven't watched TV. They haven't travelled. usw.

Nachdem die Schülerantworten vorgetragen wurden, können die den beiden Ausgangstexten zugeordneten Sätze auf dem Arbeitsblatt mündlich oder schriftlich vervollständigt werden.

● Lösungen
1. *Halim has not/hasn't played any computer games.*
2. *Kamara has not listened to rock music.*
3. *Halim has not read any detective stories.*
4. *Kamara and Halim have not/haven't travelled. They have not met people from other countries. They have not eaten Italian food.*
5. *Kamara has not learned to read and write.*

2. They have never ...
Die Schüler werden aufgefordert, Dinge zu nennen, die Kamara und Halim wahrscheinlich noch nie gemacht haben:
L: *Kamara has never been to school. Halim und Kamara have never bought a comic.*
Die beiden unterstrichenen Sätze werden an die Tafel bzw. auf den OHP geschrieben.
L: *Think of some more things that they have never done and write them down.*
(In diesem Kontext sollte die Frage *What else haven't they done?* vermieden werden, um zum einen keine sprachliche Verwirrung zu stiften und zum anderen, weil die Frage unnatürlich wäre).
In Gruppen oder mit einem Partner werden Ideen gesammelt. Außer den angegebenen Strukturen sind zusätzliche Wortangaben hilfreich, z. B. *seen, had, used, been, cinema, disco, plane, phone, hamburger.*

Mögliche Antworten:
Die Lernenden sollten dazu angehalten werden, beim Sprechen die Kurzformen zu gebrauchen.
They have never seen a car/plane; had an ice-cream, a holiday; used a phone/video recorder; been to the cinema/a swimming pool.
Die Antworten werden vorgelesen. Anschließend werden die Sätze auf dem Arbeitsblatt mündlich oder schriftlich vervollständigt.

● Lösungen
2. *They have never watched TV.*
3. *Kamara has never been to school.*
4. *They have never had a holiday.*
5. *Halim has never ridden a bike.*
6. *Dave has never got up at four in the morning.*

And you?
L: *I'm like Dave. I've never got up at four in the morning. Have you? There are lots of things I've never done. For example, I've never been/flown in a helicopter. I've never eaten Indian food. What about you? I've never ...?* (Die Struktur wird angeschrieben).
S1: *I've never seen a desert/ridden on a horse/camel/...*
Nachdem einige Schüler geantwortet haben, werden in Gruppen- oder Partnerarbeit Ideen gesammelt. Die Lernenden sollten ermutigt werden, nach unbekanntem Wortschatz zu suchen bzw. zu fragen.

A 26

Present perfect: already – not yet

1. Life in India and Britain
Die Übung verdeutlicht die Bedeutung von *already* und *not yet.* Sie kann im Klassenverband, in Einzel- oder Partnerarbeit, mündlich und/oder schriftlich durchgeführt werden. Man sollte darauf achten, dass beim Sprechen die Kurzformen gebraucht werden.

● Lösungen
7.30: *Kamara and Halim have already had breakfast. Dave has not finished breakfast yet.*
8.30: *Halim has already gone to market. Dave has not arrived at work yet.*
17.00: *Halim has already done the shopping. Dave has not done the shopping yet.*
18.00: *Halim and Kamara have already eaten. Dave has not had his tea yet.*
23.00: *Halim and Kamara have already gone to bed. Dave has not gone to bed yet.*

2. And you? What about today?
Die Schüler verwenden *not yet* und *already,* um Aussagen über sich selbst zu machen, z. B.
I haven't watched TV/had lunch/... yet.
I've already ridden my bike/played a game/...

A 27

Present perfect: Has/Have ... yet?

1. It's ten to six
Die Fragestellung mit *yet* wird anhand der Personen in A 26 geübt. Zunächst denkt der Lehrer an eine beliebige Uhrzeit und fragt, ob Dave, Kamara oder Halim wohl schon mit einer bestimmten Tätigkeit fertig sind, z. B.:
It's ten to six in the morning. Has Dave got up yet? (Antwort: *No, not yet*).
It's five past seven. Has Halim gone to market yet? (No, not yet).
It's a quarter to nine. Have Halim and Kamara had breakfast yet? (Yes, they have).
Die Aufmerksamkeit wird kurz auf das Merkkästchen gelenkt und die Bedeutung von *yet* in Fragen erklärt.
Anschließend übernehmen die Schüler die Lehrerrolle und stellen vier Fragen an ihre Partner: sie nennen beliebige Zeitpunkte und fragen, ob Dave, Halim oder Kamara schon mit einer bestimmten Tätigkeit zu Ende sind. Dabei dienen die Fragestruktur und Antwortmöglichkeiten auf dem Arbeitsbogen als Hilfestellung, z. B.:
It's nine o'clock in the morning. Has Dave arrived at work yet?
It's a quarter past six in the evening. Have Halim and Kamara eaten yet?
Go on:
In Partnerarbeit werden die Fragen 1–6 gestellt, beantwortet und ausgefüllt.

● Lösungen
1. *Has Halim gone to market yet? – No, not yet.*
2. *Have Kamara and Halim had breakfast yet? – Yes, they have.*

3. *Has Dave arrived at work yet? – No, not yet.*
4. *Has Dave done the shopping yet? – No, not yet.*
5. *Have Halim and Kamara eaten yet? – No, not yet.*
6. *Have Halim and Kamara gone to bed yet? – Yes, they have.*

An die Partnerarbeit kann ein lehrerzentriertes Gedächtnisspiel angeschlossen werden: Nachdem die Lernenden einige Minuten Zeit gehabt haben, sich die Texte auf Blatt A 26 einzuprägen, werden diese zugedeckt und die Fragen aus dem Gedächtnis beantwortet. Für jede richtige Antwort gibt es einen Punkt.

A 28

Present perfect: ever – never

1. Have you ever ...?
Der abgebildete Dialog veranschaulicht die Bedeutung von *ever* und *never.* Er kann mit verteilten Rollen vorgelesen werden. Der Lehrer demonstriert, wie der Ausgangsdialog mit Hilfe des im Kästchen angegebenen Wortschatzes variiert werden kann, z. B.:
- *Have you ever been to Britain?*
- *Yes, once.*

Auf die verschiedenen Antwortmöglichkeiten sollte hingewiesen werden:
- *Yes, lots of times/lots of them.*
- *Yes, a few/a few times.*
- *Yes, once.*
- *No, never.*
- ... (z. B. *Yes, I loved it/when I was in ...; No, never. I hate ...*)

In einem nächsten Schritt schreibt jeder Schüler acht Fragen nach dem vorgegebenen Muster in die dafür vorgesehenen Freiräume. Die Lernenden sollten ermutigt werden, eigene Ideen einzubringen und nach unbekanntem Wortschatz zu suchen oder zu fragen.
Anschließend stellen sich die Schüler ihre Fragen in Partnerarbeit und beantworten sie. Die Aufmerksamkeit wird auf die Satzstellung von *ever* gelenkt.

2. Never
Jeder Schüler schreibt auf der Grundlage der obigen Befragung drei Dinge auf, die sein Partner noch nie getan hat. Die Ergebnisse werden der Klasse vorgetragen.

A 29

Present perfect: for – since

1. I haven't washed my face for a week/since Christmas
Der Lehrer demonstriert die Übung und führt unbekannten Wortschatz ein, indem er Kärtchen mit zwei Satzanfängen und vier Satzenden zur Wahl an die Tafel heftet, z. B.:

I haven't washed my feet		*since my birthday.*
	for a year.	
I haven't had tea with Prince Charles		*since Tuesday.*
	for three weeks.	

Mit den Kärtchen bildet er zwei Sätze, z. B.:
I haven't washed my feet for a year.
I haven't had tea with Prince Charles since Tuesday.

Jeder Schüler schreibt einen ähnlichen Satzanfang auf einen Papierstreifen. Die Lernenden können die Vorschläge auf dem Arbeitsblatt verwenden oder eigene Ideen einbringen. Die Streifen werden so gefaltet, dass man den Satzanfang nicht lesen kann.
Jeder Schüler tauscht seinen Streifen gegen den seines Partners oder anderen Gruppenmitglieds aus und fügt ein Satzende hinzu, das mit *for* oder *since* anfängt.
Die vollständigen Sätze werden der Klasse vorgelesen.
Der Merkkasten fasst die Bedeutungen von *for* und *since* zusammen.

2. Holidays
Um den Gebrauch von *for* und *since* zu festigen, wird ein Gespräch vervollständigt. Die Übung kann mündlich und/oder schriftlich durchgeführt werden.

● Lösungen
Herr Adler: *For two weeks.*
Frau Adler: *We've been in Scotland since the middle of July.*
Herr Adler: *Yes, we've been in Britain since the beginning of July.*
Mrs McCraig: *What! You've been here for so long!*

Variante:
Die Lernenden können versuchen, ähnliche Gespräche selbst zu entwickeln, indem sie Personen und Orte auswechseln. Folgendes Gesprächsmuster ist hilfreich:
How long have you been in ...?
For/Since ...
Do you like it?
...

3. „seit"
Der im Englischen und Deutschen unterschiedliche Gebrauch der Zeiten und die Bedeutungen von *for* und *since* werden beim Übersetzen deutlich.
1. *Ich habe mein Fahrrad seit Mai.*
2. *Peter ist seit einem Jahr hier.*

„seit" + Präsens *for, since + present perfect*

4. A joke
Farmer: These are the best eggs we've had for years.
Woman: Then please give me some you haven't had for so long.

A 30

‚Present perfect' und ‚simple past' im Vergleich: Aussagen; Verneinung

Der unterschiedliche Gebrauch von *present perfect* und *simple past* in Aussage- und Verneinungssätzen wird anhand von Zeitungsschlagzeilen und -berichten herausgearbeitet. Für Schlagzeilen, die lediglich feststellen, **dass** etwas passiert ist, verwendet man für gewöhnlich das *present perfect,* die im folgenden Bericht angeführten Details (wann? wo? wie?) hingegen stehen im *simple past.*

1. Headlines
Die Schlagzeilen können folgendermaßen eingeführt werden:

L: *Sometime you'll probably go to an English-speaking country. You'll want to know what's happening/going on there, so you'll look at the newspapers. Let's see how much you can understand.*

Im Klassenverband oder in Partnerarbeit, mündlich und/oder schriftlich versuchen die Schüler, die Schlagzeilen auszuformulieren.

● Lösungen
1. *A pop star has bought a castle for a children's home.*
2. *A Chinaman has broken the world record.*
3. *A girl has won a trip to Australia.*
4. *There has been an accident in Central London.*
5. *Helpers have pushed some whales back into the sea.*
6. *A woman has walked across America – on one leg.*

Die Schüler können versuchen, die Regeln selbst zu erarbeiten, z. B.:

L: *Which tense did we use for all these headlines?*
S1: *The present perfect.*
L: *Why?* (Hilfestellung: *To give details about something that has happened or just to say that something has happened?*)

Der Merkkasten und der Merksatz fassen diese Funktion des *present perfect* zusammen.

2. Details
Im ersten Teil dieser Übung sollen die auf die Schlagzeilen folgenden, nähere Einzelheiten angebenden Sätze durch Hinzufügen eines Verbs im *simple past* vervollständigt werden.

● Lösungen
a) *At seven o'clock last night Maria Gomez arrived in San Fransisco.*
b) *Last Sunday about a hundred people helped to push some whales back into the Pacific.*
c) *Last night Li Peng broke the world discus record.*
d) *A pop star bought a castle in Romania last week.*
e) *Last night five people died in an accident.*
f) *Fourteen-year-old Jennifer Bailey was the happiest girl in her school yesterday.*

Which story goes with which headline?
Im zweiten Teil der Übung sollen die die näheren Umstände erklärenden Sätze den Schlagzeilen zugeordnet werden.

● Lösungen
1. d 2. c 3. f 4. e 5. b 6. a

3. Writing newspaper articles
Die in den Übungen 1 und 2 präsentierten Funktionen des *present perfect* und *simple past* werden einander gegenübergestellt, indem die Schüler die vorgegebenen Schlagzeilen als Einführungssätze der Zeitungsartikel im *present perfect* ausformulieren und die nachfolgenden, die näheren Umstände enthaltenden zweiten Sätze im *simple past* halten.

● Lösungen
1. *Manchester United has won the football cup. They won it last night at Wembley.*
2. *The actor, Robin O'Neil, has died. He died in an accident in Edinburgh.*
3. *Eighteen-year-old Sandra Wilmot has written a bestseller. She wrote it in three months.*

4. Translate these sentences

● Lösungen
1. *Peter didn't do his homework yesterday.*
2. *Peter hasn't done his homework yet.*
3. *I haven't been to Britain yet.*
4. *I didn't go to Britain last year.*

Gestern (1) und letztes Jahr (4) sind die Signalwörter für den Gebrauch des *simple past.*

Look at these sentences
Um die unterschiedliche Verwendung von *hasn't* und *didn't* deutlich zu machen, werden zwei Sätze einander gegenübergestellt.

● Lösung
b) *tells us that the visit is over.*

5. I've done it – I did it yesterday
Die in dieser Einheit geübten unterschiedlichen Funktionen des *present perfect* und *simple past* werden durch ihre Verwendung in Minigesprächen deutlich: *present perfect,* um das Gespräch zu eröffnen, *simple past* für weitere Details, z. B. Zeitangaben.
Zwei Partner oder Gruppen von 4–5 Schülern bekommen einen Pack Wortkarten, bestehend aus mehreren Satzanfängen (*I've* ...) und den dazu passenden Reaktionen (... *ago/last* ...). Jeder Schüler erhält die gleiche Anzahl von Satzanfängen und Reaktionen, die jedoch nicht einander zugeordnet sein dürfen.
Ein erster Schüler liest einen seiner Satzanfänge vor, z. B.: *I've been to Italy.* Der Schüler mit der passenden Reaktion antwortet mit seiner Wortkarte *(Me, too. I went last year)* und beginnt dann die nächste Unterhaltung mit einem eigenen Satzanfang:

S1: *I've been to Italy.*
S2: *Me, too. I went last year. I've ...*

Bei lernschwächeren Schülern liegen die Karten offen, ansonsten können sie verdeckt bleiben.
Vorschläge:

Satzanfänge	**Reaktionen**
	Me, too:
I've been to Italy.	*I went there last year.*
I've been to a pop concert.	*I went to one last week.*
I've been on a plane.	*I went on one two years ago.*
I've been on TV.	*I was on three weeks ago.*
I've seen Tower Bridge.	*I saw it last October.*
I've lived in New York.	*I lived there for six months.*
I've ridden a horse.	*I rode one last summer.*
I've had a cheese ice-cream.	*I had one three days ago.*
I've eaten fish and chips.	*I ate some last year.*
I've learned to use a computer.	*I learned it four years ago.*
I've played baseball.	*I played last August.*
I've written a story.	*I wrote one last weekend.*
I've met an English person.	*I met one last Spring.*
I've watched an English film.	*I watched one last night.*
I've read an English magazine.	*I read one two days ago.*
I've written a letter in English.	*I wrote one last Saturday.*
I've painted a picture.	*I painted one a few days ago.*

I've bought a ticket for the football World Cup.	*I bought one ages ago.*
I've played tennis with Martina Hingis.	*I played with her last Sunday.*
I've won a race.	*I won one six months ago.*
I've stayed at the Hilton hotel.	*I stayed there a few weeks ago.*

Variante:
Fortgeschrittenere Schüler können sowohl die Satzanfänge als auch die darauf folgenden Reaktionen variieren. Sie bekommen lediglich die Strukturen als Vorgabe:
– *I've …*
– *Me, too. I … ago/last …*

A 31

‚Present perfect' und ‚simple past' im Vergleich: Fragen

Die unterschiedlichen Funktionen von *present perfect* und *simple past* in Fragen werden anhand eines Fragebogens verdeutlicht. Ist das Augenmerk eher auf die Gegenwart gerichtet, stellt man die Fragen im *present perfect;* liegt das Hauptinteresse eher auf der Vergangenheit, gebraucht man das *simple past.*

1. Why are you here?
Als Einstieg zur Erarbeitung des Fragebogens könnte die Frage gestellt werden, welche der Londoner Sehenswürdigkeiten die Lernenden schon kennen bzw. von welchen sie schon gehört haben.
Dann wird jede Frage des Fragebogens einzeln vom Lehrer vorgelesen und beantwortet. Der Lehrer kann entweder selbst Antworten vorschlagen oder die Klasse bitten, sich in die Lage der deutschen Schulklasse in London zu versetzen und Antworten zu geben. Zu diesem Zeitpunkt werden jedoch noch keine Einträge in den Fragebogen gemacht.

L: *The first thing Pauline asks is, 'Why have you come to London?' What do you think the class says?*
S1: *For a holiday.*
L: *Yes, probably. Don't put a cross/write on your sheet yet, though. And then she wants to know, 'How did you get here?' What do you think? By air?*
S2: *No. By train.*
S3: *Or by coach.*
L: *Yes. Probably by train or by coach. The plane's too expensive and pupils don't usually have cars, do they? Next Pauline asks, Have …?*

In dieser mündlichen Phase braucht sich die Klasse nicht unbedingt auf jeweils eine zutreffende Antwort einigen. Sollten einige der Sehenswürdigkeiten noch unbekannt sein, kann man Schüler bitten, in häuslicher Arbeit Informationen zusammenzustellen und ggf. Bilder mitzubringen. (z. B. in Reisebüros erhältliche Kataloge).

Variante:
Fortgeschrittenere Schüler können ihre Äußerungen ergänzen, z. B.:
3. *Have you been here before?*
Yes, in 1992/last summer. I came with my parents/ a friend/…
4. *Why did you come before?*
For a holiday. I wanted to see …/live in London/wanted to improve my English/…

Nach dieser mündlichen Einführungsphase wird der Fragebogen in Partnerarbeit beantwortet. Zuerst füllen beide Partner in Stillarbeit ihre Bögen aus. Dabei können die Antworten durchaus voneinander abweichen. Danach stellt Partner A alle Fragen und B liest seine Antworten vor. Anschließend werden alle Fragen von Partner B gestellt und von A beantwortet.

2. Questions
Die Regeln für die unterschiedlichen Funktionen von *present perfect* und *simple past* werden von den Lernenden selbst erarbeitet. Die im Fragebogen enthaltenen Fragen werden in zwei Listen sortiert:

***Questions in the** present perfect* *Why have you come to London?* *Have you been here before?* *How long have you been here?* *What have you seen so far?*
***Questions in the** simple past* *How did you get here?* *Why did you come before?* *When did you arrive?* *What did you like best?*

Im Klassenverband, in Gruppen- oder in Partnerarbeit werden aus diesen zwei Listen die Schlussfolgerungen gezogen:

Bei diesen Fragen interessieren wir uns eher für die ☒ a) Gegenwart ☐ b) Vergangenheit
Bei diesen Fragen interessieren wir uns eher für die ☐ a) Gegenwart ☒ b) Vergangenheit

3. Make your own questionnaire
Um den unterschiedlichen Gebrauch von *present perfect* und *simple past* in Fragen zu festigen, sollen die Lernenden selber einen ähnlichen Fragebogen erstellen. Sie können die auf dem Arbeitsblatt erscheinenden Fragen übernehmen und auch eigene hinzufügen.

Variante:
In Projektarbeit können englisch sprechende ausländische Gäste befragt werden. Anschließend lassen sich die verschiedenen ausgefüllten Fragebögen auswerten.

A 32

Some, any: Aussagen; Verneinung

1. Our classroom
Zunächst wird der Gebrauch von *some* in Aussagesätzen und in der Bedeutung von „einige" kurz in Erinnerung gerufen. Die Schüler werden aufgefordert, ihr Klassenzimmer auf Englisch zu beschreiben. Dazu benutzen sie die Strukturen *There is a …* bzw. *There are some …*, z. B.:
There's a teacher, door, map stand, washbasin, poster …
There are some boys, girls, chairs, windows, postcards …

2. Yesterday Johnny went shopping
Im nächsten Schritt wird der Unterschied zwischen *some* und *any* in Aussage- und Verneinungssätzen deutlich gemacht. *Some* wird in der Bedeutung von „einige" und „etwas" verwendet. Zuerst beschreiben die Schüler unter Verwendung von *some*, was Johnny eingekauft hat. Es wird nur die kurze, natürliche Antwort *Some* ... erwartet.

● Lösungen
Some sweets, coke, beans, jam, cake, biscuits, yoghourt.
Sätze 1–7:
Ein Vergleich mit der Einkaufsliste zeigt, dass Johnny einiges vergessen hat:
He didn't buy any apples, cheese, tea, milk, bread, coffee.
Das Merkkästchen erinnert an die Bedeutung von *not any* = kein, keine.

Write seven sentences like this:
He bought some (sweets, coke, beans, jam, cake, biscuits, yoghurt), but he didn't buy any (apples, cheese, tea, milk, bread, coffee).

3. Could you go shopping in Britain?
In Partnerarbeit werden die zwei Listen zusammengefügt.

● Lösungen
a can of beans. (Das im amerikanischen Englisch übliche *can* ersetzt immer mehr *tin* im britischen Englisch).
a loaf of bread
a carton of orange juice
a bottle of milk
a packet of biscuits
half a pound of cheese
a jar of jam
a bar of chocolate
two pieces of cake
a tin of apricots
Anschließend können die Schüler in Partnerschaft kleine Einkaufsszenen üben und vorspielen, wie schon durch die Sprechblasen angeregt.

A shopping game
In einem Gedächtnisspiel werden die Ausdrücke für bestimmte Mengen wiederholt.
Schüler A erwähnt einen Artikel, den er eingekauft hat.
Schüler B wiederholt ihn und fügt einen weiteren hinzu usw.
Wer etwas falsch wiederholt bzw. sich nicht mehr erinnern kann, muss ausscheiden.

A 33

Some/-body,/-thing: Bitten und Angebote

In dieser Einheit werden *some, -body, -thing* in Fragesätzen geübt, mit denen die beiden Sprechakte: „bitten" und „anbieten" ausgeführt werden, z. B.:
Can somebody (someone) help, me, please? (Bitte)
Would you like some chocolate? (Angebot)

1. Asking for help
Als Einstieg in das Thema *Asking for help* bieten sich ganz natürliche Klassensituationen an. So kann z. B. der Lehrer die Klasse bitten, verschiedene Tätigkeiten auszuführen:

L: *Can somebody/someone open the door, window/clean the board/write the word '...' on the board/tell me the English for '...'/lend me a biro, some paper, felt-tips, fifty pfennigs/put these books on my desk/help me with these books/..., please?*

Die dem Einstieg folgende Übung kann im Klassenverband, in Einzel- oder Partnerarbeit, mündlich und/oder schriftlich durchgeführt werden.

● Lösungen
1. *Andy: "Can somebody lend me an atlas, please?"*
2. *Carol: "Can somebody lend me a ruler, please?"*
3. *Diane: "Can I borrow something to write with, please?"*
4. *Mike: "Can somebody give me some paper, please?"*
5. *Hassan: "Can I have something to drink, please?"*
6. *Lisa: "Can I have something to eat, please?"*
7. *Mary: "Can somebody lend me some felt-tips, please?"*
8. *Alison: "Can I listen to some of your CDs, please?"*

Zusätzlich kann man die Schüler weitere Beispielsätze zur Regel auf dem Arbeitsblatt vorschlagen lassen.

2. Politeness
Some (-thing) in Fragesätzen kann nicht nur wie in den vorausgegangenen Beispielen den Sprechakt „bitten" ausdrücken, sondern auch „Angebote machen". Die im vorliegenden Schritt verlangte Übersetzungsaufgabe soll diesen zweiten Sprechakt verdeutlichen.

● Lösungen
1. *Can I get you something to drink?*
2. *Would you like some chocolate?*
3. *Shall I tell you something interesting?*

Es kann erklärt werden, dass bei Fragesätzen mit *any* eine Ablehnung des Angebots erwartet wird, etwa:
Would you like anything to eat? (= I hope not!)
Would you like something to eat? (= I'm willing to get you something).

A 34

Any: Fragen

1. My ideal room
Die Anwendung von *any* in Fragesätzen wird durch eine visuelle *information gap*-Übung wiederholt. Der Lehrer stellt sich sein Traumzimmer vor. Dabei kann es sich um ein privates oder ein Klassenzimmer handeln. Er bittet die Schüler zu erraten, was sich darin befindet. Die ermittelten Gegenstände, Tiere oder Menschen werden mit einfachen Strichzeichnungen eingetragen, z. B.:

L: *I'd like a different (class)room. With lots of nice things in it. Can you guess what? Ask me, Are there any books?* (Der Satz wird aufgeschrieben). *Are there any posters? Or chairs or tables?*
S1: *Are there any animals in it?*
L: *Yes, my cat. She's sitting on a chair in the middle of the room.* (Zeichnet)
S2: *Are there any pictures?*
usw.

Anschließend übernimmt ein Schüler die Lehrerrolle und versucht, sein ideales Privat- oder Klassenzimmer in analoger Art und Weise an die Tafel bzw. auf den OHP zu zeichnen. Seine Klassenkameraden stellen Fragen wie im obigen Beispiel.

Variante:
Das vom Lehrer gezeichnete Zimmer bleibt verdeckt. Die Schüler müssen nicht nur die darin befindlichen Gegenstände erraten, sondern auch versuchen, mit Hilfe der Lehrerinformationen selbst auf ein vom Schülerbogen unabhängiges Blatt zu zeichnen, z. B.:
S1: *Are there any posters?*
L: *Yes, two.* (Zeichnet sie, aber so, dass die Schüler das Bild nicht sehen können). *One on the left and one on the right.*
Jeder Schüler zeichnet die beiden Poster in die entsprechenden Stellen seines Extrablattes.
L: *Now what else? Are there any …?*
S2: *Are there any chairs?*
usw.

My ideal room
Anschließend zeichnet jeder Schüler sein ideales Privat- oder Klassenzimmer in den linken Kasten seines Arbeitsblattes. Jeweils zwei Partner befragen sich dann gegenseitig über ihre Zimmer wie im obigen Beispiel. (Selbstverständlich können die Schülerzeichnungen einfacher ausfallen als die vorgegebenen Zeichnungen auf dem Arbeitsblatt.) Partner A darf das Bild von Partner B nicht sehen.
Zuerst stellt Partner A seine Fragen und versucht, mit Hilfe der gewonnenen Informationen die Zeichnung seines Mitschülers in den rechten Rahmen des Schülerbogens zu reproduzieren.
A: *Is there a bed?*
B: *Yes, on the left.*
(A zeichnet das Bett in das rechte Feld ein).
A: *Are there any chairs?*
B: *Yes, one. On the right.* (A zeichnet es ein).
usw.
Nun vergleichen Partner A und B ihre Zeichnungen, indem sie diese offen legen. Dann befragt Partner B Partner A zu dessen Bild.

Das Merkkästchen ruft die Regel noch einmal in Erinnerung: *any (-body, -thing)* wird in Fragesätzen nur bei echten Informationsfragen verwendet.

2. Is there anything on tonight?
In dieser Übung unterhalten sich zwei Partner über einen Ausschnitt aus einer englischen Fernsehprogrammzeitschrift. Abwechselnd stellen sich Partner A und B Fragen 1–5. Fortgeschrittene Schüler können ermutigt werden, kleine Dialoge zu entwickeln und später der Klasse vorzutragen, z.B.:
1. A: *Is there anything on tonight?*
B: *Yes, there's a football match at half past eight.*
A: *Oh no. I don't want to see/don't fancy that. Is there anything else?*
2. A: *Are there any films on?*
B: *Yes, Casablanca.*
A: *Oh no. I've already seen that three times.*
3. A: *Is there anything about animals?*
B: *Yes, there's 'Wild Life' at half past six. Why? Do you like animals?*
A: *Yes. I love nature programmes.*
usw.

A 35

Many, not many, not much, a lot of, lots of

1. Danger! Help!
Die Struktur *there aren't many* wird durch einen Sachtext über bedrohte Tiere wiederholt. Ein Merkkästchen ruft die Bedeutung von *many* und *not many* in Erinnerung.

Variante:
Der Absatz *Did you know?* kann als Ausgangspunkt für einen kleinen Exkurs über bedrohte Tiere dienen, z. B.:
L: *Which animals or birds are in danger today? Do you know?*
In Gruppen- oder Partnerarbeit wird mit Hilfe eines Wörterbuchs eine Liste zusammengestellt, z. B. *bats, bears, camels, crocodiles, elephants, gazelles, gorillas, hummingbirds, monkeys* (einige Arten), *parrots, orang-utans, otters, rhinos, seals, sharks, turtles, whales, wolves, zebras.* Bei fortgeschritteneren Schülern können die Gründe erörtert werden.

2. Why are these animals in danger?
Anhand des ersten Satzes kann der unterschiedliche Gebrauch von *not many* und *not much* aufgezeigt werden (vgl. Merkkästchen).

● Lösungen
Many fish are in danger because there isn't much clean water.
There aren't many pandas because there isn't much food for them.
There aren't many gazelles in Africa because there isn't much grass left.
There aren't many elephants because there aren't many forests left.

3. Not many forests, but lots of roads
In dieser zweiten Übung werden *not many* und *not much* noch einmal kontrastiert. Hinzu kommt *a lot of* und *lots of.*

● Lösungen
1. *There aren't many fields.*
2. *There aren't many forests.*
3. *There isn't much/a lot of land for animals.*
4. *There isn't much/a lot of land for children to play.*
5. *There isn't much/a lot of clean water to swim in.*
6. *There are many/a lot of/lots of roads/houses/schools/factories/…*
7. *There is a lot of traffic.*

Can I do anything to help?
In einem weiterführenden Projekt können die Lernenden ermutigt werden, Informationen über bedrohte Arten zu sammeln. Sie können auch an verschiedene Organisationen schreiben.

4. What do you know about deserts?
Jeder Schüler schreibt zwei Sätze über Wüsten auf, die mit den angegebenen Strukturen beginnen, z. B.:
There aren't many plants/animals/people/towns/schools/…
There isn't much water/rain/traffic/…
Die Sätze werden der Klasse vorgelesen.

A 36

How many?/How much?/A little/A few

1. How much do you know about the world?
Der Gebrauch von *How many?*, *How much?* und *only a little* wird mit Hilfe eines Fragebogens klar gemacht. In Partnerarbeit stellen sich die Schüler jeweils alle sieben Fragen und notieren die Antworten, die nicht immer miteinander übereinstimmen müssen. Erst nach diesem doppelten Durchgang gibt der Lehrer die Lösungen bekannt. Voneinander abweichende Schülerantworten können in fortgeschrittenen Klassen besprochen werden, wobei die Lernenden ermutigt werden, nach unbekanntem Wortschatz zu fragen bzw. zu suchen.

● Lösungen
1. *Germany: About 76 million.*
2. *About five thousand million.*
3. *Five continents: Africa, America, Asia, Australia, Europe.*
4. *Five oceans:* (in abnehmender Reihenfolge ihrer Größe) *Pacific Ocean, Atlantic O., Indian O., Southern O., Arctic O.*
5. *Lots – nearly three quarters.*
6. *Lots – about a third (166,241,000 sq.km).*
7. *Lots – nearly one eighth.*

2. What do you think?
Drei weitere Fragen machen den Gebrauch von *a few* deutlich. Wie in Übung 1 stellen sich zwei Partner jeweils alle drei Fragen und notieren die Antworten. Erst nach diesem doppelten Durchgang werden die Antworten besprochen.

● Lösungen
1. *Lots – about one kind every day.*
2. *Lots – about 70,000.*
3. *Only a few – about 150*
(verglichen mit ca. 5,000 im Amazonas-Gebiet).

3. Test your general knowledge
Der Unterschied zwischen *fewer than* und *less than* wird durch vier *general knowledge*-Fragen deutlich gemacht. Jeder einzelne Schüler versucht, die Fragen zu beantworten. Anschließend werden die Antworten der Klasse vorgelesen.

● Lösungen
1b) *The United Kingdom has fewer people than Germany. (UK ca. 56mill. Germany ca. 76.6mill.)*
2a) *The USA has more than 40 states. (50)*
3a) *One mile is more than one kilometre. (1 mile = ca. 1.6 km)*

A 37

Steigerung von Adjektiven: -er; not as ... as

Um die Struktur *-er than* kurz in Erinnerung zu rufen, bieten sich Vergleiche zwischen zwei verschiedenen Schülern an:
L: *I want two people to come out to the front.*
Look, (Susanne) is taller than (Michael).
(Michael) is shorter than (Susanne).

Die Struktur wird durch weitere ähnliche Vergleiche gefestigt.

1. Me and my friend
Angeregt durch weitere Vokabelangaben wie *long, old, young, good at* vergleichen sich die Schüler mit ihren Klassenkameraden.
Die Merkkästen erinnern an die Komparativbildung durch Hinzufügen von *-er* und an die Ausnahme *good – better.*

2. Compare these things
In einem weiteren Schritt wird die Steigerung mit *not as ... as* wiederholt und die Komparativbildung nach *-y*, die Verdoppelung der Konsonanten bei *big and hot* sowie die unregelmäßige Form *worse* geübt. Die Bildung dieser Formen wird in zwei Merkkästchen zusammengefasst.
b) *The Empire State Building is higher than the Eiffel Tower. The Eiffel Tower is not as high as the Empire State Building.*
c) *India is hotter than Sweden. Sweden is not as hot as India.*
d) *Eleven thirty-two is earlier than twenty-seven minutes to twelve. Twenty-seven minutes to twelve is not as early as eleven thirty-two.*
e) *English/maths is easier than English/maths. English/maths is not as easy as English/maths.*
f) *School on Saturdays/School in the afternoons is worse than school in the afternoons/school on Saturdays. School on Saturdays/School in the afternoons is not as bad as school in the afternoons/school on Saturdays.*

Anmerkung: Im britischen Englisch werden ein- und zweisilbige Adjektive zunehmend mit *more* gesteigert, d.h. *more cheap, more easy.*

3. Can you compare these things?
Die folgenden zwei, bei Vergleichen üblichen Strukturen werden geübt: *-er than, not as ... as.*
In Gruppen gebrauchen die Lernenden den angegebenen Wortschatz, um Vergleiche anzustellen, die auch ungewöhnlich oder lustig sein dürfen. Fortgeschrittene Schüler können eigene Ideen hinzufügen.

Mögliche Vorschläge
Trains are faster than motor bikes/Motor bikes are slower than/not as fast as trains.
Camels are slower than motor bikes.
Walking is better/healthier than going by car/
Going by car ist not as healthy as walking.
A month is shorter than a year.
Ice-cream is colder than coffee.
Winter is colder than summer.
February is earlier than June.
Girls are better at English than boys.
usw.

A 38

Steigerung von Adjektiven: -est; -est/-er

1. Who is the tallest?
Um die Struktur *the ...-est* zu wiederholen, bieten sich Vergleiche im Klassenzimmer an. Die Fragen sollten gebündelt gestellt werden wie im folgenden Musterdialog, damit die Schüler auf eine natürliche Art und Weise antworten können. Würde nämlich jede Frage einzeln gestellt, wäre die natürliche Antwort nur der Name der betreffenden Person, z. B.: *Who is the tallest? – Alex.*

L: *Look at all the people in this room. Some are tall, some are short. Some have long hair, some short. Who's the tallest? And the shortest? And who has the longest hair; And the shortest hair?*
S1: *(Alex) is the tallest.*
S2: *(Birgit) is the shortest.*
usw.

Anschließend werden die Lernenden aufgefordert, mit Hilfe der angegebenen Strukturen ähnliche Aussagen über ihre Familien zu machen, z. B.:

My grandfather is the oldest in our family.
My sister has the longest hair (biggest feet/loudest voice ...)
I'm the best at sports/English ...
My aunt's the worst swimmer.

2. How much do you know?
Im Klassenverband machen die Schüler Aussagen über ihr eigenes Land, z. B.:

The biggest city/longest river in Germany is ...
I think the nicest place(s) is/are ...

Danach werden Fragen 1–6 in Einzel- oder Partnerarbeit beantwortet.

● Lösungen
1. *Death Valley is the hottest place in the world.*
2. *Siberia is one of the coldest places in the world.*
3. *Mexico City is one of the biggest/dirtiest places in the world.*
4. *The Himalayas are the highest mountains in the world.*
5. *The Nile is the longest river in the world.*
6. *The cheetah is the fastest animal in the world.*

3. Do you know?
Nachdem die Superlativform der Steigerung isoliert geübt wurde, erscheinen nun Komparativ- und Superlativformen zusammen. Die Übung kann im Klassenverband, in Partner- oder Gruppenarbeit durchgeführt werden.

● Lösungen
1. *The Eiffel Tower is higher than the tower of Pisa. The Empire State Building is the highest.*
2. *The Sphinx is the oldest. The Parthenon is older than the White House.*
3. *Steve is better than Peter at maths. But Peter is better than Steve at English. Ann is the best at maths. But she is worse than Peter at English. Peter is the worst at maths.*

A 39

Steigerung von Adjektiven: more ... than; just as ... as

1. Places
Anhand zweier Bilder von Bonn und New York wird die Komparativbildung mit *more ... than* in Erinnerung gerufen. Es können auch andere Städte oder Ortschaften miteinander verglichen werden.
Der angegebene Wortschatz dient als Impuls für einen mündlich ausgeführten Vergleich, z. B.:

New York is more international than Bonn.

Es bietet sich auch eine Wiederholung der Struktur *not as ... as* an, z. B.:

Bonn is not as international as New York.

Bei fortgeschritteneren Lernenden können die Aussagen diskutiert werden. In einer anschließenden Gruppenarbeit versuchen die Schüler, ähnliche Aussagen zu Städten und Ortschaften ihrer Wahl zu machen.

2. What's more difficult?
Das Mustergespräch führt die Strukturen *What's more ...?* und *just as ... as* ein. Die Schüler lesen die anschließenden Fragen durch und versuchen, mit Hilfe des angegebenen Wortschatzes einige ähnliche Fragen aufzuschreiben. In einem nächsten Schritt werden in Partnerarbeit alle Fragen zuerst von Partner A, dann vom Partner B gestellt. Es ist wichtig, die Schüler mit natürlichen, kurzen Aussagen antworten zu lassen und sie nicht zu unnatürlichen, vollständigen Sätzen zu zwingen, z. B.:

A: *What's more difficult – geography or history?*
B: *History, I think/For me, history.*

Auch in dieser Phase können fortgeschrittene Schüler die Aussagen diskutieren.

What do you think?
Nach der mündlichen Übung macht jeder Lernende einige schriftliche Aussagen über sich selber.

Anmerkung: Im britischen Englisch werden ein- und zweisilbige Adjektive zunehmend mit *more* gesteigert, d. h. *more cheap, more easy.*

A 40

Steigerung von Adjektiven: the most; the -est

1. The most interesting?
Die Superlativbildung mit *the most* und *the ...-est* wird anhand zweier Lehrerfragen *What's the most interesting place you know?* und *What's the most exciting book you've ever read?* wiederholt. Nachdem einige Schüler im Klassenverband diese Fragen beantwortet haben, schreibt jeder Lernende eigene, ähnliche Fragen auf einen Zettel. Es folgen mehrere Vorschläge auf dem Arbeitsblatt, es können aber auch eigene Ideen eingebracht werden.
Entweder im Klassenverband oder in Gruppenarbeit werden die Fragen gestellt. Der Schüler, der antwortet, stellt jeweils die nächste Frage. Fortgeschrittene Schüler können die Antworten auch diskutieren.
In einem weiteren Schritt schreibt jeder Schüler drei Sätze über sich selbst, die alle mit *The most* anfangen, z. B.:

The most interesting place I know is ...
The most exciting film I have ever seen is/was ...
Jeder trägt seine drei Sätze der Klasse vor.

2. Let's make some advertisements
Die Anwendung der zwei Superlativformen *the most* und *the ...-est* wird anhand von Werbetexten geübt.
In Gruppen- oder Partnerarbeit versuchen die Lernenden, die Texte durch Superlativformen der passenden Adjektive zu vervollständigen. Dabei kann es für jeden Text mehr als eine Möglichkeit geben.

● Lösungen
1. *Why buy the most expensive ...*
2. *The fastest way to better English*
3. *The most beautiful/exciting girls use ...*
4. *The warmest jackets for the coldest days*
5. *We have the most modern/greatest computers*
7. *The greatest/most exciting show you've ever seen!*

A 41

Could: Vorschläge; Vergangenheit (Möglichkeiten, Fähigkeiten, Erlaubnis)

1. Making the world a better place
Der durch *could* ausgedrückte Sprechakt „Vorschläge machen" wird im Kontext von Umweltproblemen verdeutlicht. In Gruppen- oder Partnerarbeit werden mit Hilfe des angegebenen Wortschatzes einige Vorschläge zur Vermeidung von Umweltschäden gesammelt. Die Lernenden sollten ermutigt werden, nach unbekanntem Wortschatz zu suchen bzw. zu fragen. Anschließend werden die Vorschläge der Klasse vorgelesen.

Mögliche Vorschläge:
We could/ People could
recycle (more) things/glass/paper.
collect glass/paper.
use glass/paper again.
use/buy recycled paper.
wrap presents in newspaper/recycled paper.
have showers, not baths.
stop buying plastic bags/things in plastic boxes.
take shopping bags with us (when we go shopping).
walk to school/work.
go to school/work by bike/bus/train.
use/buy electric cars.
share cars.
have more buses and trains.
have/build towns without cars.

2. The good old days
In diesem zweiten Schritt wird die weitere Funktion von *could* und *couldn't*, vergangene Möglichkeiten und Fähigkeiten auszudrücken, geübt, z.B.:
She could play in the streets. She couldn't take the shopping home by car. (Möglichkeiten)
She could drive a tractor when she was ten. (Fähigkeit).
In Partner- oder Gruppenarbeit werden die beiden auf dem Arbeitsblatt angegebenen Listen in zwei Kategorien eingeteilt: *She could ...* und *She couldn't ...*

● Lösungen:
She couldn't take the shopping home by car.
She could play in the fields.
She could swim in the rivers.
She couldn't go anywhere by car.
She could drive a tractor when she was ten.
She couldn't buy many new clothes.
She couldn't train for a job.
She could ride a horse when she was eight.

And you?
Mit Hilfe des vorgeschlagenen Wortschatzes schreiben die Lernenden ein paar Tätigkeiten auf, die sie früher schon beherrschten bzw. nicht ausführen konnten.

Die Schüler können daran erinnert werden, dass *could(n't)* auch „dürfen" bzw. „nicht dürfen" bedeuten kann. Das kann in ihren Aussagen zum Ausdruck gebracht werden, z.B. *I couldn't go to pop concerts until I was ...*

Mögliche Antworten:
I could use a cassette recorder/play the flute/ride a bike/ski/swim/take photos/... when I was about (ten).
I couldn't buy my own clothes/use a computer/do algebra/speak English/... until I was about (thirteen)/until a few years, months ago.
Zum Abschluss liest jeder Schüler zwei seiner Sätze vor: *I could ...; I couldn't ...*

Variante:
Fortgeschrittene Schüler können sich über die Aussagen unterhalten, z.B. um Hintergründe zu erfahren:
– *I couldn't use a computer until a few months ago.*
– *Why not? Didn't you have one at home?*
– *No. But then my friend got one and she showed me.*

A 42

Have to; would like to

1. Rosa has to work, but she would like to go to school
Die Bedeutungen von *have to* und *would like to* werden im Zusammenhang mit der Beschreibung einer brasilianischen Familie verdeutlicht: zum einen, was sie tun müssen, und zum anderen, was sie tun möchten.
Zunächst liest der Lehrer die Einleitung vor und erklärt den unbekannten Wortschatz. Danach werden die Sätze in Partnerarbeit vervollständigt. Anschließend lesen einzelne Schüler ihre Sätze vor.
Die Formen von *have to* sowie die Bedeutungen von *have to* und *would like to* werden in Merkkästchen zusammengefasst.

● Lösungen:
Rosa's mother has to cook, clean and make bread to sell in the market. But she would like to have enough money to send her children to school. Rosa has to sell her mother's bread. But she would like to go to school. Rosa's father and brother have to work in the fields. But her father would like to work in an office and her brother would like to get a job in a city.

2. Do you have to ...?
Die Strukturen *Do you have to ...?* und *I have to ...* werden in Partnerarbeit geübt. Die Frage wird zunächst von Partner A, dann von Partner B gestellt, z. B.:

A: *Do you have to help at home?*
B: *No, not much / Yes, I have to do the shopping and take the dog for a walk.*

Anschließend berichtet jeder Schüler der ganzen Klasse über die Antwort seines Partners:

A: *(Michael) doesn't have to help at home.*
B: *(Susanne) has to look after her baby sister.*

don't / doesn't have to
Eine Übung zu den Verneinungsformen *don't/doesn't have to* schließt sich an. Wie oben befragen sich die Partner gegenseitig darüber, was sie zu Hause nicht machen müssen:

A: *What don't you have to do?*
B: *Cook, the washing and the shopping.*

Anschließend berichten einzelne Schüler der ganzen Klasse über die Antworten ihrer Partner:

A: *(Andy) doesn't have to cook, do the washing or (do) the shopping.*

Der Merkkasten fasst die Bildung der Frage- und Aussagesätze mit *have to* sowie die hier geübte Bedeutung von *have to* (Verpflichtungen) zusammen.

A 43

Must(n't); have to

1. You must do this – you mustn't do that!
Der Gebrauch von *must* und *mustn't* wird durch Gebote, Verbote und Warnungen in Schule und Elternhaus verdeutlicht. Die Lückentexte können entweder im Klassenverband, in Partner- oder Einzelarbeit ausgefüllt werden.

● Lösungen
His teacher says:
1. 2. 3.: *You must do your homework/listen to me/work harder.*
4. 5. 6.: *You mustn't be late for school/eat in class / forget your books.*

His mother says:
1. 2. 3.: *You must go to bed earlier/show me your homework / always tell me where you're going.*
4. 5. 6.: *You mustn't come home late/eat so many sweets / watch TV all day.*

What else does his teacher or his mother say?
In einem zweiten, freieren Schritt versuchen die Schüler, in Gruppenarbeit einige Ge- und Verbote zusammenzustellen.

Merkkästchen:
Das erste Merkkästchen nennt nicht nur die Funktion von *must,* sondern weist auch darauf hin, dass dieses modale Hilfsverb meist von Autoritätspersonen gebraucht wird, ansonsten aber sehr autoritär klingt. In der Umgangssprache wird anstatt *must* meistens *have to* verwendet.
Das zweite Merkkästchen macht besonders auf die für deutsche Lernende unerwartete Bedeutung „nicht dürfen" entgegen „nicht müssen" aufmerksam.

2. Have to
Translate these sentences
Dieser Schritt verdeutlicht, dass für die Vergangenheit und Zukunft nicht *must,* sondern nur eine Form von *have to* verwendet werden kann. Im Klassenverband, in Partner- oder Einzelarbeit werden die Sätze 1–3 ins Englische übersetzt. In die rechte Spalte wird die jeweilige englische Entsprechung von „müssen" notiert.

1. Ich musste gestern zum Zahnarzt
   I had to go to the dentist's yesterday.
2. Ich werde noch einmal hingehen müssen.
   I'll/will have to go again.
3. Mein Bruder hat noch nie zum Zahnarzt gehen müssen.
   My brother has never had to go to the dentist's.

musste
had to
werde ... müssen
'll/will have to
hat ... müssen
has (never) had to

Auf der Grundlage der obigen Sätze wird folgende Regel erarbeitet:

> Für die **Vergangenheit** und **Zukunft** brauchen wir *have to* (nicht *must*).